W9-BAE-253

The Stone Soup Book of
Friendship Stories

The
STONE
SOUP
BOOK
of

FRIENDSHIP STORIES

BY THE YOUNG WRITERS
OF *Stone Soup* MAGAZINE

Edited by
WILLIAM RUBEL, GERRY MANDEL,
& MICHAEL KING

CHILDREN'S ART FOUNDATION
Santa Cruz, California

The Stone Soup Book of Friendship Stories
William Rubel, Gerry Mandel, and Michael King, editors

Copyright © 2012 by the Children's Art Foundation

All rights reserved. No part of this book may be reproduced in any manner whatsoever without written permission from the publisher.

Stone Soup Magazine
Children's Art Foundation
P.O. Box 83
Santa Cruz, CA 95063

www.stonesoup.com

ISBN: 978-0-89409-012-7

Book design by Carl Rohrs
Typeset in Brioso
Printed in the U.S.A.

ABOUT STONE SOUP

Stone Soup, the international magazine of stories, poems, and art by children, is published six times a year out of Santa Cruz, California. Founded in 1973, *Stone Soup* is known for its high editorial and design standards. The editors receive more than 10,000 submissions a year by children ages 8 to 13. Less than one percent of the work received is published. Every story and poem that appears in *Stone Soup* is remarkable, providing a window into the lives, thoughts, and creativity of children.

Stone Soup has published more writing and art by children than any other publisher. With our anthologies, we present some of the magazine's best stories in a new format, one designed to be enjoyed for a long time. Choose your favorite genre—friendship, animal, fantasy, historical—or collect the whole set.

Contents

THE WINDS OF AFRICA

by

ABBIE GUNN

age 13

Breeze turned her face toward the sun. The hot, dry air blew up from the savannah, blowing her sandy hair around her cheeks. She reached up and snatched the hair, hastily sliding it into a hair tie. She glanced toward the sun, and just as it seemed to touch the high anthill she sprinted across the African grassland. She ran and ran, the grass hissing to the side as she sprinted through it. Soon she reached the anthill. She leaped into the air, grabbing a bright red blossom from the flamboyant tree, and scrambled skillfully to the top of the red pile of dirt. She did all this with ease for she had done it almost every day for the past seven years.

When she reached the top, she balanced herself, and, rising to her full height, she waved the red flower high in the air. Soon she could see Akwakwa's figure skirting across the waving grass. Breeze slid down the anthill. She tossed the flower aside and reached up to her hair. She pulled out her hairband and shook her head.

She closed her eyes and thought of the first day she had met Akwakwa. Breeze had been only seven. She had been climbing the flamboyant tree which still stood beside the ant-hill when Akwakwa had suddenly appeared below her. Excited to have found a friend, Breeze yelled a greeting. From that moment on they had been good friends. They had arranged the signal of waving the flower, knowing that Breeze would have finished her homework and that Akwakwa would have finished her chores by that time.

Breeze came out of her daydream when the grass's sighing turned into moaning with Akwakwa's approach. When Breeze opened her eyes, she saw Akwakwa quickly tucking her *chitenge* back around her waist. Akwakwa raised her head and smiled. Breeze returned the smile, thinking as always of how beautiful Akwakwa was.

Akwakwa's skin was soft and her big brown eyes were very deep and full of life. Breeze thought that her lips were perfectly shaped, even though they were considered too small for the likings of the other villagers. Her nose was oval and slightly turned upwards. Akwakwa broke the silence by asking, "Would you like to go to the river?"

"Sure," replied Breeze in a happy tone. In fact, that was exactly where she had wanted to go. Somehow, Akwakwa always knew where to go.

"Let's race," added Breeze.

Breeze stepped beside Akwakwa as another dry wind blew. Both turned to face the small river which had formed during the rains.

"Ready, steady, GO!" shouted Breeze. They leapt forward and ran with all their might; they ran as if they were never going to stop, past the bunch of eucalyptus trees in which they had built a small treehouse kingdom, hurtling over bushes and fallen logs. Their feet pounded on the hard, dry ground, creating little puffs of red smoke. Soon they were running on smooth, hot rocks. It made them step more daintily, as if they were walking on needles. Suddenly they both stopped, for they had reached the river. They turned to face each other.

"Another tie," puffed Akwakwa.

"Another tie," echoed Breeze as she waded into the water and lowered herself onto a smooth rock. Akwakwa followed and when both were relaxed she asked, "How was your day?"

"Pretty normal. I can't wait until our long break!"

"Why? I thought you liked school."

Breeze couldn't help smiling. It was such an innocent question. "I do, it's just, well, it gets boring and so routine. I need a change."

"I think I understand. Sometimes I wish I was still young so that my grandmother wouldn't always be reminding me to act grown up. She says that I need a husband. This is the only time when I am free to act what is in my heart."

"I know what you mean, my mother is very picky. She is constantly telling me to sit up straight, not to bite my nails, not to put my elbows on the table. The list goes on forever. Would you please hold my hands, I want to dip my head in."

Akwakwa rose and took Breeze's hands in her own. Breeze leaned back, letting her hair dip into the water. The cool water swirled and jumped as if angry that something had come in its way. It cooled Breeze and relaxed her. She tightened her grip on Akwakwa and leaned further back.

"I'm starting my initiation ceremony tomorrow," mumbled Akwakwa.

"What?" asked Breeze as she jerked her head from the water.

"I'm starting the initiation ceremony tomorrow," repeated Akwakwa.

Breeze sighed. She looked out into the waving grass.

Without turning her head she said, "You'll be gone for over two weeks, you'll go away from the village to live with an old woman. You'll have to do backbreaking work. Then you'll have to go to a ceremony where they'll cut your forehead to put medicine in and then they'll knock your two front teeth out. You don't really want that." Turning back she asked, "Do you?"

"They don't knock people's teeth out anymore," stated Akwakwa defensively.

Breeze sighed again. "I'm sorry," she said, "It's just that I'll miss you, and after your initiation ceremony it won't be long until you get married."

"Don't worry. My grandmother says I'm too childish for any man to want. No ceremony can change what's in my heart."

"I sure hope not."

"Come, let us walk to the sun."

Breeze smiled and stood up, "OK, let's run!"

"To where?"

"Nowhere! Just run toward the sun. Ready, steady, GO!"

The girls ran and ran, each heading toward the sun. They ran with the grass whipping their legs. They ran so long that it seemed forever and still they ran. When they finally stopped, the sun was low in the sky.

"Akwakwa, I don't know what I'll do without you," sighed Breeze.

"I won't leave you!" yelled Akwakwa, exasperated.

"You've got to marry sometime," stated Breeze matter-of-factly.

"You've got to go to boarding school sometime," shot back Akwakwa.

Breeze looked away. "I've gotta go home," she whispered, and with that she ran away.

"Meet me in two weeks!" shouted Akwakwa to Breeze's back.

When the time came, Breeze was overjoyed. She still had three weeks of her school vacation left and it had been exactly two weeks since she had last seen Akwakwa. The day had slowly dragged by. Finally, it had been time to go watch the sun. As she stood there, she hopped from one foot to the other, thinking that the sun had never moved slower. At last the sun touched the anthill.

Breeze reached the anthill in record time. She shinnied up it and almost fell off when she waved the red flower.

When she got down she didn't wait for Akwakwa but went to meet her. When the two reached each other, they hugged, rocking back and forth and smiling with joy. When Breeze finally pulled away, she suddenly noticed the rings of copper on Akwakwa's neck. Her eyes quickly traveled to Akwakwa's wrist and then to her ankle. Both had silver chains on them. As Breeze's eyes surveyed Akwakwa she saw that Akwakwa had a new *chitenge* and earrings as well. Akwakwa's smile faded. "You were right," she whispered. Breeze only stared. "Come, let us play, for this will be the last time."

At this Breeze found her voice. "When are you getting married?" she inquired.

"In five days, but I must start preparing tomorrow," answered Akwakwa.

"Let's go to the kingdom," was all Breeze said.

The girls sat with their legs dangling over the edge. The sun was big and hot and as they sat the sun warmed them with a tingly feeling which made them feel drowsy. There was no joyous chatter between them as usual. Finally Breeze asked, "What's he like?"

"He has a large farm with many cattle and..."

"I don't care whether he's rich or not. I want to know

what he's like! I don't want you married to some idiot who will beat you!"

"He's very nice, I have known him a long time although I have only seen him about ten times because he lives about twenty kilometers away…"

At that Breeze gasped, "I'll never see you again."

"I know," replied Akwakwa, biting her lip to keep from crying.

"We have to go visit all of our favorite spots," cried Breeze as she grabbed hold of a branch and swung down.

The rest of the afternoon went by in a blur. The sun had set and the first star appeared when it was time to part. They embraced each other for a long time, both trying hard to hold back their tears.

Breeze stepped away and looked into Akwakwa's brown eyes. They were not dancing with excitement as usual but steadily looking back at Breeze.

"Do not cry, for this day will live as long as we live, for I know that it is in both of our hearts. Once something is in your heart it never leaves." With those words Akwakwa hugged Breeze once more and then ran into the darkness. Breeze watched her disappear as a dry African wind blew her hair onto her cheeks, their childhood days carried away by the winds of Africa.

Rebellion

by

Abigail Goutal

age 13

I was going to kill Justin.

How had I ever let him talk me into this? I did not want to join a writing club, I did not need to join a writing club... So why was I standing outside this classroom, trying to convince myself to open the door and walk in? Because I was idiot enough to show my best friend a handful of peculiar poems.

Inside, eleven uninteresting and disinterested faces—and a couple of others—turned toward me. I stood self-conscious-ly in front of them, feeling an uneasy twinge deep down some-where. One of the girls stood up after a minute and stepped forward. She was pretty the way my sister's old Barbie dolls were pretty—artificial, nondescript. She set my teeth on edge.

"Hi, I'm Kelly. Welcome to Writer's Circle. What's your name?" It reminded me of the message on an answering ma-chine. I told her my name, nervously.

"Guys," said Kelly in a voice that positively sparkled, "this is Evan."

"Hi," I heard in twelve different inflections, overlapping and blending into a sort of bubbling sound. They introduced themselves, one after another. Sarah. Tyler. Renee...

"We were just about to hear this fabulous story Tina wrote," twinkled Kelly. "Why don't you have a seat and listen in, since you weren't here."

"Fabulous... " As I sat down, I remembered my conversation with Justin the other day. He had used the same word.

"Evan, these are fabulous," he told me after reading them intently.

I shrugged. "Not really. They're weird. I don't even know what they mean."

"Kid, give yourself a break. They're terrific."

"Thanks." I was still skeptical.

"You know," he remarked, handing them back to me, "there's a writing group after school. They're meeting this Friday. In room 312, I think. You should check it out."

"I don't think so. I'm really not all that good."

"Sure you are. Just try it once, then decide."

"You can cancel at any time, and the free gift is yours to keep," I mocked. "You sound like a TV commercial."

"C'mon, Evan. I'm serious."

"Fine. You be serious. I'm going to the library. I've got homework to do."

But I did think it over. Justin never insists on anything he doesn't think is important—which is partly why I like him. If he took my weird, self-confusing, punctuationless, poemish things that seriously, then I supposed I could give it a shot.

Which was how I found myself sitting after school on Friday in room 312, biting my fingernails into numbness while I listened to Tina's "Mayflowers."

Tina was a thin, big-eyed, shy-looking girl about my age, maybe a little younger. She read in a silvery, barely audible voice and kept nervously playing with one earring. And when she finished, they were all over her.

"I guess it was OK," said someone, Tyler maybe, "except hardly anything happened."

"And, no offense, Teeny," Dan didn't look as if he particularly cared if she was offended, "but Marisa was sort of a wimp, y'know?"

"Dan," a girl protested quietly.

"And what about Darren—how come he didn't stand up for himself?" That was Emily, I thought, putting in her two cents.

"Good description," the same girl broke in, obviously trying to salvage something of Tina's self-esteem. It didn't seem to work. Tina was close to tears.

The criticism kept coming relentlessly. The dialogue was unrealistic. The characters were old-fashioned. And stereotypical. And boring. The plot was shaky. And so on and so on and so on. Finally, they let up.

"Anybody else?" asked Kelly brightly.

Silence. Tina's woebegone, little-girl face made me want to stand up for her, but I was a newcomer and my opinion wouldn't count for much.

"Evan, did you bring some writing with you?" Michelle asked me.

"Uh... sort of... yeah," I said reluctantly.

Well, can we hear it?" Kelly asked very patiently. Her tone infuriated me. Without answering, I dug in my pocket, pulled out the crumpled sheets, sorted through them, and came up with the one both Justin and I liked best. Smoothing it out, I started hesitantly to read.

> in the glimmer-wet pond
> quivering dark-green depths
> engulf amoeba children...

Kelly looked like she was about to interrupt. I rushed on through the poem, through the journey to the mysterious sand-swirled bottom of the pond, describing the eerie un-heard song of the amoeba children.

When I finished, Tina's tears had evaporated. She leaned forward as if she was waiting to hear the rest. Her hands twisted tightly around the edge of her chair. Several of the others looked distinctly interested.

Kelly's smile was disdainful. "What was that, anyway?"

"It was a poem," Tina said in soft surprise.

"It didn't make sense."

"Amoebas don't have children," Jon told me smugly, "they divide."

I blinked, wondering when this had turned into a science lesson and why anyone would care in a poem.

I had puzzled them into a few seconds of breathing space, evidently, but now the same barrage of disapproval that had crushed Tina came crashing down on me. What was "glimmer-wet" supposed to mean? What was the "true silence"? And, most of all, what was it all about?

Suddenly Tina's supporter snapped, "Knock it off, you guys!"

Silence rushed like space into the room.

"Sarah," Kelly said in a voice that was two parts scorn, one part annoyance, and one part pure astonishment.

But now Tina was on her feet. "You make such a big deal out of 'constructive criticism.' All you ever do is put people down, and I'm sick of it! Just sick!"

"Look," said Sarah in a more reasonable tone, "all she's saying is, you could be more supportive."

"Who's running this group!" said Kelly heatedly.

Ha, she's getting mad! I am given to snap judgments, which I know is not good, but Kelly really was obnoxious.

"You said 'Mayflowers' was fabulous before," I pointed out.

"I did not," she said nastily, darting a glance at Dan.

Now, I can put up with a lot of things, but that isn't one of them. I lost it.

"Those were your words. 'This fabulous story Tina wrote.'" I mimicked her sugary tone venomously. "We all heard you. Even if it might be awfully convenient to forget."

"He's right, Kel," Sarah put in.

"I should know what I said, shouldn't I?"

"That's exactly what I mean," I snapped. What was she, some kind of nut? Did she get a kick out of trashing people's best efforts?

"I don't know about the rest of you," said Tina shakily, "but I'm leaving. This is a joke!"

"And you're a quitter," Kelly spat.

"Just because we're not all Miss America material," Sarah said levelly, "doesn't mean we can't have our own opinions. Tina doesn't think this is a good thing any more, and she has a right to leave. And so do I." She took Tina's hand and turned to go.

"Just because we don't like some dumb story…" Jon began, unwisely. Tina turned on him.

"Who asked you?"

Adam intervened. "Oh, leave her alone. I'm sick of arguing. I quit. Evan, you coming?"

"Absolutely!!"

Melissa got to her feet slowly. "Me too. Sorry, Kel," she added, "but I think they're right."

The five of us left, not looking back.

Outside in the quiet hallway, we were silent, thinking, Did we just do what I thought we did? Finally, to break the tension, I suggested, "Why don't we start our own writing group?"

They stared.

"You know," Melissa murmured, "It just might work."

"Why not?" said Sarah. "A Misfits' Circle. I mean, you know, Tina writes these old-fashioned *Anne-of-Green-Gables*-type romances, like 'Mayflowers,' and Adam is into way-out science fiction that nobody can follow..."

"Shows how much you know," he teased. Sarah flashed him a metallic grin.

"...and I write fifty-six-page-long stories about elves and princesses and evil spells and stuff, and Melissa does these infinitely gloomy murder mysteries set in Romania or New Zealand or wherever."

"And I write scientifically inaccurate poetry that doesn't make sense," I concluded ruefully. "A writing club for weirdos."

"Yep, that's us," Tina giggled, "the Literary Loony Bin."

Whereupon we all cracked up, and we stood there in the school hallway for a quarter of an hour, laughing like drunken hyenas and thinking up crazy names for ourselves, until somebody—it might have been Melissa —said, "The Amoeba Children."

And all of us agreed that was just about perfect.

"Didn't I tell you, kid?" Justin said for approximately the thirty-seventh time.

I groaned, giving him a half-hearted push. "OK, Justin. OK. You were right. But not like you thought."

"Well..."

"Well what?" I demanded.

"Part of it was getting Tina out. Don't get me wrong, now, I meant it about your poems. But I wanted her out... it wasn't good for her."

"You know Tina?"

"Sister."

"What?"

"Yeah." Justin grinned unconcernedly at me.

"For crying out loud!"

"Exactly! Sometimes she'd come home literally in hysterics because they were so rough on her. And every time she managed to miss a meeting, they'd be twice as bad at the next one. Especially what's-her-name... Kelly?"

"Kelly. I can just imagine."

"So that's why I pushed you so hard to go. I figured you'd pick up on what was happening and wouldn't stand for it. And it's a lot easier for Tina to take action if she's got someone behind her."

Well, gee.

"Listen, tell Tina I liked her story. 'Mayflowers.'"

Justin smiled.

"I'll tell her."

LINDY

by

ARI RUBEN

age 11

I used to cringe each time our doorbell rang. Nine times out of ten the person on the other side of the door was Lindy, the girl from a few houses down the street.

"Can you play today?" she'd ask.

"No, I'm doing homework," I'd say, even if I wasn't.

"Can I help your mom with the baby?" she would ask next.

Before I could say no, there was my mom inviting her inside again.

"Where's the baby?" Lindy asked. She asked that same question every time she walked inside the house. And the answer was always the same.

"He's in the family room," my mom would say, smiling as she watched me silently mouthing the words along with her.

My baby brother, Kelly, liked Lindy. He liked her a little too much, if you asked me. He'd squeal and laugh when she made silly faces at him or tickled his feet. To make matters worse, whenever Lindy played with Kelly, she'd take out every one of his toys. You can guess who would have to put them away later on.

While she was busy with Kelly and my mom, I'd sneak out of the room. But no matter where I went, Lindy soon found me. It was as though she had radar. "I'm bored," she'd say.

Why don't you go home then? I thought to myself, but I never could say it out loud.

Most of the time she would just stand there and stare at me until I asked her to play Nintendo. She would talk and talk all through the game, especially when it was my turn to play. She talked so much that it ruined my concentration. I lost a lot of lives that way.

If she had not been such a pest, I might have liked her visits. After all, she was quite pretty. And she always let me be the first person to sign her casts. Usually ten-year-old girls like flowers and silly stuff like that, but Lindy thought my pictures of black widow spiders were pretty cool.

I remember drawing my first spider. That was the day I met Lindy. I had wanted to bring some interesting insects to school the next day but found only two sow bugs in my own yard, and one of them was dead. I put both of them in a shoe box. I decided the pickings had to be better around the neighborhood. Instead, I was the one who got picked.

"Hey, boy with the glasses, what are you doing?" Lindy yelled.

"Looking for bugs. Got any good ones?" I answered even before I spotted her sitting on her front step.

"I don't know. We just moved here last week," said Lindy. "I'll help you find some bugs, but first you have to sign my leg cast."

Since I was getting quite desperate for bugs, I agreed. Neither of us had anything to write with, so I went home to get a marker. My mom said I could borrow her red and black pens as long as I returned them and didn't get the ink on my clothes.

I decided to make a drawing of a black widow spider because it was the only thing I could think of that is red and black and pretty easy to draw. Lindy liked it. She said it looked almost real. (When Lindy broke her arm a couple months later, I drew two black widows. And the time she broke her finger, I made an itsy-bitsy spider.)

Then she asked if she could see my bugs, so I opened the lid of the shoebox. When I looked inside, I couldn't believe my eyes. Next to my two sow bugs, Lindy had placed two stink bugs, a ladybug, and a couple tasty-looking leaves for all of them to eat.

"We do have some good bugs here after all," laughed Lindy.

I thanked her for the surprise. It was almost dinner time, so I said goodbye to Lindy and told her to come over to my house sometime.

The problem was Lindy wanted to be at my house all the time. She was always hanging around my house. I used to ask my mom, "Why doesn't she stay at her own house?"

"Maybe she likes you," my mom would say. Then she laughed when I scrunched my nose. That would get me madder.

Sometimes Lindy wouldn't even have to ring the doorbell for me to know she was around. One time I got a strange feeling and looked out the window. Guess what I saw. Yes, it was Lindy. She was helping my dad wash his car.

I liked helping my dad wash the car, but I didn't want to do it with Lindy there.

"She has a family. Why does she also need ours?" I asked my dad when he finally came in the house.

"Now, be nice," my dad said.

I didn't like that answer.

One day, not so long ago, I went outside to get the mail from the mailbox. I saw two patrol cars parked outside Lindy's house. I was curious, so I sneaked around some bushes and waited.

Two policemen came out of the house. Lindy was with them. Her mother came out of the house. She was crying. Then two more policemen came out of the house. They had her stepfather in handcuffs.

"He didn't mean to hit her that hard," yelled Lindy's mother.

Lindy wasn't crying, though. She was just talking (as usual) to the cops. They opened the police car and she started to get in. Then she spotted me.

"He's my best friend," she told one of the officers as she pointed directly at me. Then she smiled and waved.

I waved back. And I kept on waving as the patrol cars sped away and out of view.

The doorbell doesn't ring too much anymore. But when it does, I run to get there first. I am always hoping it will be Lindy.

BEST FRIENDS

by

DARBY LACKEY

age 11

The sound of my keys against the doorknob sounded as loud as a bunch of kids having a party in the silence of the night. As quietly as I could, I pushed open the door and switched on the light. Dropping my keys on the foyer table, I cast a desperate glance around my apartment with its messy floors, overflowing bookshelf, and walls covered with papers and posters. I needed to clean! Opening my top desk drawer, I began to separate the wrinkled papers into different piles.

Suddenly, my eye caught on the corner of an envelope with the name Tina scrawled in messy green ink. Slowly, I picked up the letter with trembling fingers, then held it tight to my chest and closed my eyes, letting warm memories flood over me.

It had been a night just like this one. We were riding in the back of the car, I don't remember where. Tina and I were gazing with awe at the beautiful night sky. The clouds were one shade of black, and the sky another, but you couldn't tell them apart.

"Girls, time to go to sleep," Mom called softly from the front seat. "Quietly! Sam's asleep," she added, indicating the small, sleeping boy on her lap.

Soft as mice, Tina and I snuggled down under the warm covers. I gratefully laid my head on the downy pillow. My eyes were almost closed when I surprised myself by asking, "Tina, who's your best friend—in the whole world?"

"You!" she answered. Then, "Who's yours?"

"You," I answered, without a moment's hesitation.

"I guess that makes us even, huh?" Tina asked in a soft voice.

I nodded and we both slept soundly, happily content with each other's company.

The sound of the corner of the envelope hitting the hardwood floor jerked me back to reality. Without noticing the tears that were rolling down my cheeks in rivers, I gently put the envelope back in the drawer and pulled out a clean sheet of stationery. Taking a pen, I sat down at the desk and began to write: "Dear Tina…"

THE SUNRISE

by

CADELBA LOMELI-LOIBL

age 13

I'm standing on the snow-covered sidewalk in front of my friend Ashley's house. It's six-forty in the morning. Ashley is standing next to me. Her tired eyes are focused on the eastern sky, and her short strawberry-blond hair is blowing in her face. It's cold outside, and I'm wearing the big black coat with fake fur inside that my mom bought me especially for this trip to Colorado.

Across the street are houses, all of them made of wood in the rustic log cabin style that I love. To the left of us are more houses, and past them the mountains, Wonderland Lake Park, and the hill we plan to climb this morning. To the right of us the sky is just beginning to glow with the orange light of dawn.

"Ashley," I whisper, "let's go. I don't want to miss too much of the sunrise just standing here."

"Right," answers Ashley, looking down at the snowy ground, "let's go."

Off we run down the sidewalk, our boots sinking in the

snow that fell last night.

You see, I've been visiting my friend Ashley and her family in Colorado for twelve days now, and today is my last day here. Ashley and I decided to make today special, by waking up early and watching the sun rise from a hill near their house.

When we had walked two blocks Ashley glanced behind us toward the rising sun.

"Yikes," she exclaimed, "we're going to miss it if we don't hurry." Ashley began to run, her feet sliding on the ice hidden beneath the snow. I followed Ashley, looking down at her patterned boot prints in the snow.

We ran for ten minutes straight. When we reached Wonderland Lake Park we both stood a moment at the trailhead trying to catch our breaths. Ashley took the first step up the mountain, and I clambered up the trail close behind her. As soon as I reached her I began to run up the trail, tripping over stones and branches. Ashley caught up with me.

"This is so cool," she panted as we ran.

"I know," I answered. "It's refreshing to be out here in the cold, and everything's so beautiful around us."

We had run about halfway up the hill when Ashley suggested we stop to rest. We walked off the trail a few feet to a little plateau and stood there looking at the sky.

"It's breathtaking," Ashley admired. "Look at those pinkish-orange clouds right there," Ashley pointed. "Those are my favorite colors."

"Oh, it's magnificent," I replied. "But my favorite color of cloud is that purplish-blue one over there." I pointed eastward.

Suddenly Ashley stiffened and put a finger to her lips.

"What is it?" I whispered.

"Look," Ashley answered in a hushed voice, pointing to a huge boulder about forty feet away from us. I followed her gaze and caught my breath when I saw the deer. There were two of them standing by the boulder. Their noble heads tilted upwards, catching our scent in the wind.

"Ashley," I spoke louder now, "there are more! Look over there, three deer by that tree, and one more behind the yellow bush!" As we looked around we realized there must be about ten deer all within a hundred-foot radius of us.

"Lucky they're does," murmured Ashley, "I wouldn't want to meet a buck up here all by ourselves."

"Maybe we should continue up the hill," I said.

"OK," replied Ashley. We walked back to the trail in silence and continued up the hill.

When we stopped again, it was because I had spotted two perfect boulders to sit on. With a word from Ashley we walked off the trail again. We sat upon the boulders and decided that we wouldn't go any farther because we could view the sunrise best from here. It was quite a magical place to be sitting. Behind us were the huge mountains, dark sky, and the still visible moon. Ahead and below us, there was Wonderland Lake Park, Boulder City, and the sun's crest seemingly rising from the sleeping city.

I checked my watch. "Seven twenty-five," I remarked to Ashley.

"See," said Ashley, "this is the actual time my dad said the sun would rise, but I think the most beautiful time is right before the sun rises."

"That's true," I answered.

Ashley and I sat on the boulder about twenty minutes longer, simply observing the sky, the sun and moon, the deer and trees, and the city. We observed life and took it all in quietly.

"Well, I guess we should go home," I said finally. The sun had risen completely by now, and the day had begun.

"C'mon," laughed Ashley, "race you down the hill!" We ran

as fast as we could. When we reached the bottom of the hill we both laughed together.

"You know," said Ashley, "next time you come, it can be on my fifteenth birthday, and we can climb up this hill and watch the sunrise again."

"Now that's a great idea!" I said.

A Time
for Hope

by

Chloe Busch

age 13

Kara Myers stared out the bus window and frowned. It had been raining ever since she left Portland and she had wanted her arrival in California to be sunny. It was amazing she was even here, the way her mother had carried on. "Don't forget anything, don't use the bathroom, don't eat anything but what I packed," and "Have your father call me the second you get to his house." She was such a worrier! Kara smiled at the expression that always came over her mother's face when she realized what she was doing. Usually they got along fine, but the last few weeks, ever since Kara had said she wanted to visit her father, had been rough.

Kara's parents had divorced when she was five. Her mother said it was because he couldn't handle being a father, but Kara sometimes wondered. When he had moved to California and married again, she had tried to forget about him, but lately he had pushed his way into her thoughts all the time. She loved his laughing brown eyes and wide mouth, even if her mother didn't. After all, he was her father and he had been very eager to have her come visit. He said she could help out with the new baby, for Diana, his wife, was pregnant. Kara loved that, she adored babies and wanted to be a pediatrician one day.

Kara woke from her daydreams and looked up. The bus was dingy and gray and there were only five other passengers besides her. One was an old black man who was practically draped over his seat. His head was leaning at an uncomfortable position against the window and he seemed to be sleeping. Kara looked at him and wondered who he was visiting. She hoped he wasn't all alone, that would be the worst way to travel, all alone.

Across from the man was a very fat woman and her young daughter. The little girl had bright red hair pulled back into tight pigtails and she was using her mother as a pillow. The woman, a platinum blond with too much makeup, was staring out the window and she looked sad. Kara wondered if the woman ever felt sorry she was so overweight, or did she even think about it?

Behind Kara was a tall thin man reading a newspaper. He had black wire-rimmed glasses on and a briefcase on the seat next to him. She wondered what he did, maybe he was a lawyer or an accountant or maybe he was a spy who dressed as a businessman to divert attention. She smiled to herself, for the man looked much too boring to be a spy.

Then Kara stopped smiling, for right across from her seat was a guy of about fifteen and he was staring right at her. Kara's heart started pounding as she looked at the boy. He was very cute, with curly blond hair and deep blue eyes. She blushed as he grinned right at her. Oh gosh, what was she going to do, the boys in her high school had never so much as looked at her, much less stared like this one. Kara looked down self-consciously but then smiled at the boy. Immediately she wished she hadn't, for he started coming over to the seat next to her! What was she going to do?

Kara blushed harder as the boy plopped his long body down beside her.

"Hi, I'm Jake, I was watching you over there and I thought I could come over and say hi. What's your name?" Kara felt like crying. He would never understand. Never in a million years. Why oh why had she come on this trip? She should have stayed home with her mother.

Frantically she looked up at the boy, who smiled down at her. He looked friendly enough, maybe he would understand. Kara lifted up her hands and began signing, "My name is Kara." Jake looked down at her with bewilderment and Kara's hopes sank. She tried again, this time just signing "Hi." But he didn't understand.

"What's wrong with...?" Jake turned his head so she couldn't see what he was saying. She wished the ground would open up and swallow her. Jake was staring at her in that way so many others had, eyes full of embarrassment and pity. For the millionth time she wished she could talk. She could explain everything to him then and make him understand. But no, Kara could never do that, she wouldn't be able to hear her words. Kara was deaf.

Slowly Jake got up and returned to his own seat, still staring at Kara. She could picture him going home and telling his friends, "I met this freak on the bus... " Oh it was more than she could bear!

Suddenly California didn't seem so great after all. The words of her mother rang in her ears, "Your father doesn't know sign language, and he can't read lips like you. What will you do in an emergency? How will you communicate? You're better off with me." Now Kara knew her mother was right. It had been silly to think that her dad would understand her. All Kara wanted to do now was go home. She leaned her tired head back on the seat and fell into a troubled sleep.

A few hours later Kara awoke and looked out the window. As unfamiliar land rushed by the whole episode with Jake came flooding back. She sneaked a look in his direction and to her surprise he was smiling at her. Kara stared groggily as he scribbled out a note on a pad of paper and passed it to her. The note said:

Dear Girl Across From Me,
I'm sorry about earlier, I was really rude. I was just surprised that you, well, you know. I've seen what you do, signing, before. I'd like to learn how to do it. Could you teach me?
                    —Someone Who Wants To Be Friends

As Kara read the note she blushed again but this time with happiness. No one had ever asked her to teach them sign language before. People usually just walked away embarrassed.

Kara turned and smiled at Jake, beckoning to him with her hand. On the pad she jotted:

I can read lips, just look at my face when you talk and I can understand.
                    —A Girl Who Would Like To Be Friends

Jake read the note and laughed, which made Kara even happier. She knew she had a friend.

Over the next few hours Kara taught Jake the whole alphabet in sign. He was a patient learner and soon they could carry on a slow conversation. Kara was thrilled.

That night, the bus reached California and its tired passengers stood to stretch their limbs. Kara looked eagerly out of the window searching for her dad. Finally she found him, with a tall pretty woman standing next to him. Then, Kara gasped and her eyes grew wide. Outside, through the bus window, her father was signing. She stared, shocked, as he said, "Welcome Kara." Then she rushed out of the bus and into his arms.

As Kara walked away with her dad and stepmom she turned back to look at Jake. He was surrounded by some other guys but he looked up and got her eye.

"Goodbye," she signed.

"See you soon," he signed back, for they had exchanged addresses and had planned to get together. Kara smiled happily and walked off with her dad. Maybe California wouldn't be as bad as she thought.

My Best Friend

by

Patrick Patterson

age 8

My best friend lived next door to me. He lived there for a very long time. His wife died before I got to meet her.

My best friend had blue eyes. He liked fishing, hunting, and hiking. He was an older man and like a grandfather so I called him Poppy.

The way I remember him when I was little was that he used to bring corn to us for our supper. The corn came from his garden. He had a very big garden.

When I was about four, we made a message sender, and one day he put donuts in it. The message sender went from my treehouse to his garden. It was a clothesline with a pillowcase on it.

We used to make things in his cellar. He had a lot of tools in his cellar. He had guns in his fishing cabinet. He let me shoot a BB gun one day. We played hide-and-seek. I'd hide in his fishing cabinet every time. I would watch him cut the heads off of fish that he caught when he went fishing. We used to pretend we were fishing in his yard. We would sit in his boat and hold his fishing poles and net.

One day I saw him taking down the cage for his dogs. I asked him why he was doing that and he said that they died. I think he was sad that day.

In his living room I made up stories from the Bible about his dogs and read them to him.

When I was five I went to kindergarten and I didn't get to play with him much. I would go over to his house after school. He would give me flowers from his flower garden for my teacher.

He would walk in the woods in the fall and get bittersweet for my mother.

When I was about six years old I joined Little League and Poppy would pitch the ball to me. He was a New York Yankees fan and my team was the Yankees.

One night when I was in second grade Poppy got sick in the night and had to go to the hospital in an ambulance. The next morning my parents and brothers and sister were talking about it and I asked what happened and my mother said that Poppy had a stroke. I didn't know what a stroke was but I knew that Poppy was very sick.

When he was in the hospital I was too little to go and see him, but I made cards and pictures for him just like I did for his refrigerator when he was not sick.

A couple of months later he moved into a convalescent home. Every Sunday we went and saw him. One day Poppy came home for a couple of hours and we showed him his garden and he knew who I was when he saw me. They asked him if he knew who I was and he said, "My best friend."

One Sunday night his son called and told my mother that Poppy died. After he died, I was very sad for a couple of weeks. I still miss him when I think about him.

Poppy died when he was eighty-four years old. I have a lot of different friends now, but they are my second best friends because Poppy was my first best friend.

MYSTERY GIRL

by

CHRISTOPHER ZANTI

age 13

Jeff smiled at the girl who sat next to him. Only a few minutes ago they had been playing against each other, now they were becoming good friends.

The girl was about twelve years old. She had blond hair and beautiful deep blue eyes. Her name was Stephanie, she went to Dorval Elementary School, and a while ago she had been playing for their handball team. Now she sat resting on a bench nursing a swollen knee. She had on a light pink shirt with the number fifteen on the shoulder, and white shorts, also with the number fifteen. Her legs, arms, and face were tanned from the sun.

Stephanie looked over at Jeff and smiled back. He pushed his brown hair out of his eyes and looked at her. She was beautiful. At least Jeff thought so. They exchanged looks and smiles for a few more seconds, but their daydreaming was interrupted by the coach who came over to Stephanie with an ice pack for her knee. He apologized for taking so long and handed her the ice pack. The coach was in his mid-forties with a few gray hairs on his balding head. Jeff had seen him before when he had come to play games at Dorval. After a minute or so, he walked off and left Jeff and Stephanie alone on the bench.

Stephanie held the ice pack on her knee as she talked to Jeff, but when they turned to watch a play in the game, it slipped off her knee and hit the floor. Jeff leaned over and picked up the ice pack for his friend. He replaced the pack on her knee and they continued to watch the game together until it was his turn to go back in.

Jeff kept thinking about how he had met this girl. Only a few minutes ago they had been involved in a very big game. The score had been tied at ten to ten. Stephanie had been tending the goal for Dorval and Jeff had been a forward for the Christmas Park team. Once the coach had blown the whistle, the game started up again. When one player from Dorval had fumbled the ball, Jeff had gotten hold of it and passed it to Jill, a teammate. She had then passed it to a big bully named Gary. (Bad mistake!) Gary wasn't just your type of guy who ate footballs, he was the type of guy who ate the people who ate footballs! He was a sports jock who just loved to show off and now was a good chance to! Gary took the ball and whipped it at Stephanie with all his might. When the ball came at her, she dove for it. She had jumped to one side and caught the ball, but when she put her leg down to regain her balance, it dislocated from being so tight from the jump lift-off. Jeff and some people from both teams came over to her when the whistle blew. Jeff looked at her knee and helped her up. He knew how much it must hurt for he too had problems with his knees and wore a brace for sports. Gary had to make some cheap shots, but Jeff ignored him. Some of the audience applauded to see someone from another team helping an opponent. Stephanie looked at Jeff and smiled, "Thank you."

Then Jeff and Stephanie had sat on the bench together, talking about the game and other things. It looked as if Christmas Park was going to win this one with only a few minutes left.

When the final buzzer sounded, the players shook hands with each other. Jeff walked back to the bench. The coach came over and shook hands with him and patted Stephanie on the shoulder, saying something about being good sports. Stephanie struggled to get up from the bench and Jeff could see her knee was really swollen so he let her lean on him and they walked slowly to the gym doors. As they approached, and as the crowd had begun to thin out, Jeff could see his mother talking to another woman. It turned out to be Stephanie's mom. The two women walked over to the two kids. After they finished talking, the four of them went outside to the parking lot. Jeff helped Stephanie into the back of the car where she could rest her leg on the seat. The two mothers shook hands. It looked like they were going to see each other again. Stephanie leaned over and put her arms around Jeff and hugged him. She whispered, "Thank you," again. Jeff stepped back and smiled at his friend. She reached into her knapsack and pulled out some paper and a pen, scribbled for a minute and handed him the piece of paper with her phone number and address. This was the beginning of a good friendship.

THE BARN

by

ELISE LOCKWOOD

age 12

It was about a year after my father died that my older brother got a job at The Barn. This converted tavern was literally a barn, torn down and renovated to make it larger, and it was here that most of the entertainment took place in our small town. It was not far away, only down the alley and across the meadow from my home. I went there frequently, mostly to visit my brother, but I would often linger, as many boys did, to observe the rough games that men enjoyed. There was one main event that attracted the most attention, if one excluded the numerous poker games and gambling that went on unaccounted for. Men would come from as far away as Portland to witness these famed matches; to witness the dog-fights.

As I stepped unnoticed into the stuffy Barn, my nose swelled with the odors of cheap beer and rolled tobacco. I was sickened as the nasty stench of drunken men filled my nostrils. As subtly as possible, I slipped past rounds of chanting and whooping gamblers, laughing insanely as their savings were lost. I made my way to the bar, where my soft-spoken brother stood a spectator. His eyes were fixed on the far corner of the crude place, where the largest group of men and boys had begun to form. I shook my head solemnly. I could hear the snarls and yelps even above the cruel jeers of the assembled audience. The dogfights had begun.

This form of entertainment brought The Barn most of its business, especially on colder fall days like this. I, like my brother, enjoyed watching the sport, though sometimes it became too sad for us to witness, for the losing dog often wound up severely maimed and more often dead. Today's fight appeared to be drawing a huge number. Curious, I crept to the edge of the crowd.

The sounds of the fight grew immensely with each step I took. I made my way closer to the action, here and there receiving pushes or shoves from the angry spectators. Approaching the ring, I immediately recognized one of the fighters. He was well known about town. The fierce pit bull rarely lost. I stood, eyes fixed on the wretched game. The pit bull struck once, then twice. The opponent, seeming somehow familiar to me, yelped in agony. Again and again the canine went in relentlessly. In mere minutes the other dog was down. Bleeding from gaping bite marks, the poor beast lay still. For a bit, the pit bull seemed to slack off, but I soon realized it was just a form of his training. Every time the wounded dog stirred, the champion was on him. Taking my eyes off the savage game for a moment, I scanned the surroundings for a familiar face. I spotted the owner of the pit bull across the ring. Even from where I stood I could sense the ferocity in his voice. Shaking my head, I continued to look for one I could call a friend. Then I spotted him.

I made one or two attempts to call out to the man, but

they were only to be drowned out by the screams of the crowd. Once again aggravating everyone around me, I fought my way through the crowd where I finally reached him.

"Mr. McGuire. What are you doing here?" I questioned. Christian McGuire, ignored by most of the townspeople and the butt of many cruel jokes, kept his back to me for several seconds. Those seconds seemed like hours for me.

He had come to our town before anyone else living here now had even heard of it. And when all the settlers came with their new lifestyles and customs, Mr. McGuire was overwhelmed. He was frightened of change, and that ruined him. He now lived up top Sutton's Hill. It was the type of place children dared each other to visit, forbidden and feared by the townsfolk. He lived much like a hermit there, and no one ever saw a glimpse of him except on rare occasions when his old dog got out. His dog…

And as he turned and faced me with tears in his eyes I knew now who that losing dog was. No wonder I thought I recognized the mutt. It was Christian McGuire's dog. My first reaction was one of utter shock. I looked at McGuire and then at the ring. In my thinking I hadn't even noticed the fight was over. Men had started to depart, finally bored of the massacre. In the midst I spotted both dogs, but one of them barely resembled a dog at all. The champion strode off with his master, and I could sense no remorse. For a while Mr. McGuire was silent. He almost seemed dead himself. The ring now completely cleared out, we entered it together. I didn't say anything, and neither did he. He knelt down, sighed, and with a swift, almost graceful movement, lifted the dog from the ground. He started walking rigidly toward the door of the barn. I walked with him.

"Why did you do it?" I hadn't realized how close to tears I was until I heard it in my own voice.

"I had to." His voice was strong, but lifeless.

"But, why? He did nothing to you. He was your companion." Christian McGuire stopped in the doorway.

"You think I wanted this?" He was quiet for a moment as he looked away. His voice was softer now. "You know what this winter is going to get like." He looked down. "I have nothing. My crops are near gone, I have no money. And no one in this town is going to be handing out loans, not to me, anyway."

"What did this have to do with the dog?" I asked impatiently. His voice was full of shame as he answered.

"About a week ago, the owner of The Barn and I made a deal. The men love to see sweet victory. You saw the bets. They were going crazy tonight." His voice was gentle. "In my pocket, I have more money than I ever had. I'll be able to survive the winter, and I'll have enough to get good crops started next year. I'll miss my old friend; I'm sorry it had to be this way."

"I'm sorry too."

He turned and left, carrying the dog in his arms. In the distance I could see Sutton's Hill.

HOLDING HANDS

by

BRETT C. YOUNG

age 12

As I put my hand down on the table, I could feel
my pinkie barely brush by his hand. Slowly, I moved my eyes
toward the hands that lay so close by each other. I tried to figure how far they were from one another, but my mind would
just not work it out. I turned my eyes back to the glowing
screen. I was glad the lights had been turned off when the
movie had started.

Slowly, I picked up one finger at a time, only moving them
not much more than a centimeter at a time until they were
right by his hand. To my surprise, he picked up his hand to
scratch his head and laid it back down on the fingers that had
just inched so slowly to that spot where they lay now.

I didn't draw back at his touch, I just sat there letting my
mind absorb the feeling of his warm hand against my cool
hand. It was an astonishment that neither of us pulled away
when our hands first touched one another.

At first, not too fast but not too slow either, we each

moved our hands until they were a knot that couldn't be untied. By that time, the film wasn't what I was thinking of, but of each movement of my hand, and everything else he did. I was all uptight except the hand he held. The rubbing thumb against the fingers he was holding was what kept that hand able to move. It was relaxing to know someone, like him, liked me.

ON THE HEADLAND

by

ABBY SEWELL

age 13

The headland was gray and deserted, almost sinister, with the heavy silver clouds gathered overhead. The only signs that it was not entirely dead were the slender girl, her golden-brown hair blowing around her face, and her black dog, who was straining forward against the leash. The two of them were walking quite close to the edge, on the mud left over from the rain of the day before.

Jen glanced down and felt a pleasurable tingle of fear in the knowledge that one wrong move would send them both keeling over the edge to meet the rocks below. Beyond the shore, the sea rolled on to the horizon in wild abandon. This was what she loved about her visits to Maine, the shore and the gray ocean, so different from her own beach at home in California. Here there was the long, lonely stretch of headland with the long, lonely stretch of sky above it and the long, lonely stretch of water below it.

The dog was less interested in the scenery than her mistress was. What she wanted was a brisk run. It was all Jen could do to keep the animal from dragging her across the headland.

"Annie! Here, girl," she called, stopping to catch her breath. Annie stopped pulling against the leash and turned her head inquiringly. Then she made a full circle and ran back toward Jen, lashing her tail. In a sudden fit of affection, she sprang up on her hind legs to put her paws on the girl's shoulders.

The impact set Jen off balance; she lost her footing and fell backwards, dragging Annie along with her. Too startled even to scream, she clamped her eyes shut and waited for the end to come.

An instant later, she landed, but not as she had expected to land. A kind ledge had broken their fall. It was just big enough to support the two of them—bits of the edge had crumbled and fallen when they landed. Jen crouched back against the side of the bank and took a firm hold on Annie's collar. She heaved a couple of sighs to relax her trembling body.

"Well," she said shakily, for Annie's benefit, "looks like we may be here for a while."

She looked up. The drop was long but not terribly steep, and there were plenty of footholds. She could get back up without much trouble if she was on her own, but what about Annie? There was no way to get the dog up, and if Jen left Annie alone on the ledge, she would probably panic and go over the edge.

"No, girl, I can't risk that. I'll stay with you until help comes." She did not say "if it comes," even to herself. It might be hours before her grandfather started to worry about them. Jen often took Annie and disappeared for most of the day, returning just in time for dinner. ("I think it's only cupboard love with both of you," her grandfather would remark cynically.) As for the chances of anyone else passing by, it was unlikely. In all her prowls on the headland, Jen had never seen another living thing, let alone a human being.

Girl and dog curled in an unhappy huddle. The sea wind was cold and damp. Now that she was no longer in motion, Jen began to shiver. The wind bit her, nipped her, tasting her like some dainty morsel put before it. She tried to squeeze Annie closer for warmth, but the dog was getting restless, and she wiggled away, sending a volley of stones crashing down. Jen pulled her back as the side of the ledge crumbled again.

Annie settled down with a soft whimper. Jen was beginning to get stiff with cold, but she did not dare to move. Her joints were creaking, but she managed to hold perfectly still. They sat that way for a long time, punctuated by Annie's whimpers. Jen allowed a few tears to wander down her face and wiped them off on her shoulder, since both of her hands were full of dog.

"I'm cold, I'm tired, I'm hungry," she said out loud. "I want to go home and take a long hot bath and then sit in front of the fire and eat gingerbread." She was about to elaborate further when an unexpected noise stopped her. It was a rhythmic *slosh-slosh*—the sound of someone walking through the mud! Annie raised her head and whined, pawing at the rocks.

"Help!" Jen's voice cracked. "Whoever you are, come help us!"

The wind that had chilled her came to her aid now. It carried her voice up to the top of the headland, and the unknown rescuer must have heard it, for the *slosh-slosh* came nearer. A moment later, a young man's face appeared at the brink of the cliff, about twenty feet above her. His cheeks were ruddy from fresh air and exercise and his face was well sculpted.

"Are you stuck?" he called down. His voice reached her faintly, since he was calling against the wind.

"In a way. I think I could get up, but I'm afraid to leave

my dog. She would have fallen already if I hadn't been holding her."

There was a muffled exclamation and then, "How long have you been there?"

"Hours and hours," she replied vaguely. Really, it could have been anywhere from twenty minutes to five hours. It had felt like five hours to Jen. She added with sudden fierceness, "And don't tell me that I should leave Annie and save myself. I won't! She's my grandfather's dog and he would never forgive me if I let anything happen to her." She would have looked almost comical, glaring up at him from her position, if either of them had been in a laughing mood.

"I wasn't going to say that," the young man said. "But I don't see how we can get her up."

Jen stroked Annie thoughtfully. Now that help had arrived, her mind was strangely clear. "I have an idea," she said, unhooking Annie's leash from her collar. The dog squirmed and barked, sensing that her rescue was near. "I'm going to throw the leash up to you, and you hold onto one end and lower the other one down to me. I think it'll reach. Do you have anything I could use to make a sling? I could tie it around Annie and you could hoist her up, see? She's not heavy. I could lift her myself, if it would do any good." She was talking so fast in her excitement that all of this came out in a jumble, but he seemed to understand her.

"A sling? What exactly do you have in mind?"

"I don't know." Annie barked again and Jen had to clutch at her to keep her from getting loose. "Don't you have anything I could use?"

"Well... Oh, of course! Why didn't I think of it right away? There's my flannel. Hold on." The face disappeared briefly and reemerged, grinning. He dropped the flannel down to Jen, who grasped it with sudden hope.

"Won't you be cold?" she asked.

"Doesn't matter. Here, throw me the leash." She tossed it up to him and he caught it neatly in one hand. One end of it came hurtling down.

Jen set to work immediately. With her left hand she held onto Annie's collar, while she tied the flannel around the dog's chest by the sleeves with her right hand and fastened it to the leash. The knots were misshapen but strong—she had not been a Girl Scout for nothing—and although the flannel was old, the material felt sturdy enough.

"OK!" she shouted up and let go of the collar.

Annie whimpered as she was hoisted off the ledge. Inch by inch, she was pulled upward. The leash strained; it swung from side to side with Annie's struggles so that one moment she would be hanging out in the open air while Jen watched, biting her lip. The next moment she would hit the side of the cliff with a thump. A seam ripped somewhere. Jen chomped down on her lip in an agony of suspense.

At last the young man was able to reach the dog and set her up beside him on the ground. Annie showed her elation at meeting solid earth by running in circles, waving her tail wildly, and covering her savior with doggy kisses. He reached down and rubbed her ears with a smile.

Jen waited to see that Annie was safe before she scrambled up, nearly losing her hold a dozen times, and dislodging half of the rocks she met. As she came within his reach, the young man gripped her arms and heaved her over the last bit. Jen plopped down, as happy as Annie was to be on the ground. Having received an enthusiastic greeting from the dog, she got to her feet, stretching her cramped muscles, and looked at her rescuer. He was massaging his arms.

"Thanks," she said. "If you hadn't come along, I might... we might..."

"No problem," he interrupted. His dark hair was matted and tousled and he smelled of sweat, but he made a splendid figure all the same. "You don't live around here, do you?"

"No, I'm visiting my grandfather, Mr. Slater." Jen looked up at him shyly and a little bit archly out of her fringed green eyes.

"We're neighbors then. I'm Dave Kelly—I'm home from college for the summer." So this was the "Kelly boy" her grandfather had talked about so often! He was not what she had expected, and she had certainly not expected to meet him this way.

Jen said suddenly, "Would you like to come to dinner? Grandfather won't mind—he'll be grateful to you forever for saving Annie."

"Sure," he said, and flashed her a grin that made her feel that it had all been worthwhile. The two humans set off along the headland, with Annie rushing ahead, still wearing Dave's flannel.

The headland was deserted once more, and the only sound was the sighing of the sea.

SUNBEAMS

by

CAROLYN NASH

age 13

The moon gazed down on me, shining brightly off
the water. The stars twinkled in the deep blue sky, each one
different from the rest. Swifts of moonlit clouds blew past the
mountains in the distance. The waves dwindled to shore, sliding up along the sand and then disappearing into the water.
The sand beneath me was cool and moist. My windbreaker
and jeans kept me warm and I had buried my bare feet in
the beach. The wind pulled and twisted my hair and I tucked
it into my shirt. My family and I had driven to the upper
peninsula of Michigan yesterday to spend time at our cottage which we had bought the previous year. It was located
on Lake Superior, where we had spent every summer since
I could remember. It was a dream to own this house, despite
the lack of running water, excepting what we got from the
lake, and the bathroom being a small outhouse nestled in the
trees. Listening to the waves rolling into shore, I felt at home,
a feeling the beach had always given to me. I closed my eyes

and listened to the wind swirl around my face.

"Hello."

My eyes flew open in surprise. He was standing by the shore, letting the waves lap at his feet and ankles.

"Hi," I answered, smiling. I was pleasantly surprised to see someone my age because a quiet beach didn't seem to appeal to that many thirteen-year-olds. "My name's Kara."

"I'm Trever. Do you have a place up here?"

"We just bought a house last year," I said, gesturing toward the cottage. "You?"

Trever looked briefly out to sea and said, "We sailed in yesterday." He pointed to a sailboat that had been pulled onto shore.

"You sail on this water?" I asked in amazement and then felt embarrassed at the obvious answer.

He nodded. "Every summer we pick a different area to visit. We spend a few days in different towns, but most of our time is spent on the lake."

"So you won't stay?" I asked in disappointment.

Trever shrugged. "I doubt it."

I thought I detected a hint of regret in his voice.

"Maybe I'll see you tomorrow," he said, starting to walk down the beach.

"Maybe." I smiled as he splashed down to the far side of the bay.

I woke up early the next morning and changed into my bathing suit for a swim. Most people think Lake Superior water is too cold for swimming in mid-July, but I had loved the cool water ever since I could swim. I eased myself into the lake, letting the waves break around me. I submerged myself in water, glided along the surface and then flipped onto

my back. For a moment my head throbbed with the cold. I rubbed my cheeks and dove under again. This time there was no pain, only the cool caress of the water.

When I finished swimming, I turned toward shore and swam a slow crawl stroke in. I wrapped my towel around me and looked up to find Trever standing by a tree.

"Hi," he said, stepping toward me.

My cheeks flushed and I wondered how long he had been there.

"Hi."

There was an awkward silence between us and I looked out to the horizon.

"My father hurt his wrist last night and he said it might be a week before he'll be able to sail."

"I'm sorry," I said.

Trever smiled. "You mean you want me to leave?"

"No... I only meant..."

Trever nodded, still smiling. "I know." He sat down in the sand and I sat beside him. His eyes were fixed on the water. His black hair was just long enough to hang in his eyes and he used a hand to brush it back. "Kara..." he stopped abruptly and then started again. "Kara, my sister, she has some kind of... she's dying."

My body froze. I wanted to reach out to Trever but the only thing I could think to say was I'm sorry, which wasn't adequate. Trever was a stranger to me and I didn't know how to respond.

"I was watching you swim and it reminded me of how she used to, before she got sick. She's quit everything. School, friends, all of it."

I knew Trever wasn't much older than I was but his face seemed sad and lonely, and he seemed older than thirteen or

fourteen.

"You remind me of her, of how she used to be. I was wondering if you might come see her. If you don't want to it's all right."

For a minute I lost my voice. I felt cold and I took a deep breath. "Can I come now?"

We walked down the beach and I could feel how nervous Trever was. He stopped at a small white cabin and led me inside.

"We're renting it for the week," Trever explained. He took me straight to the door of his sister's room, knocking gently. When no one answered, he pushed the door open and stepped inside. I hovered behind him. Sitting on a small bed was a girl with the same black silky hair as Trever. She was short and very skinny with large brown eyes that looked strained.

"Misty, I want you to meet someone," Trever said, touching his sister's arm. "This is Kara." He glanced at me and I stepped forward. Misty looked up into my eyes, a gentle, innocent glance. Her skin was deathly white. She looked no more than twelve.

"Hello," she said weakly and then turned her head to the wall.

"Hi," I answered, feeling unsure of myself.

"Misty, Kara likes to swim, like you do," Trever whispered. I could see that he was trying to get us to talk.

"I can't swim anymore," Misty answered bitterly.

"Misty?" I asked. "Would you like to come outside and see the beach?" Misty didn't answer. Trever sighed in defeat and began walking toward the door. I followed slowly.

"Yes," Misty whispered as I opened the door to leave. "I'll go to the beach."

I turned back and watched her climb out of her bed and extend her hand toward me. I took it and we walked carefully out of the room where Trever was standing.

"Trever, I'm going to the water," she said.

Trever spun around and took Misty's other arm. We led her out to the beach. It was still early morning and the sun was hidden behind the clouds. Tiny rays of light pierced through them and glittered on the water, sparkling like a sea of treasure.

"Sunbeams," Misty whispered. She turned to me and smiled. "When I was little I used to try and catch them." Slowly she began to walk toward the water. The waves danced around her feet and ankles. The hem of her nightgown touched the water's surface. Trever and I watched as she eased herself inch by inch into the water. She swam out toward the light shining brightly off the lake. Then in one graceful movement, she pushed herself forward and her laughing face was caught in a single sunbeam, sparkling down from heaven.

THE DAY THE BUTTERFLY CAME

by

KRISTIN SPARKS

age 12

He never really had a name, the Butterfly. Jenny and her grandfather had just found him there, on the windowsill.

It was a quiet day in spring, and not much was going on. Jenny was pushing her grandfather around in his wheelchair. Just as she was about to suggest they go inside, there he was, the Butterfly.

Jenny quickly wheeled her grandfather over to it. Afraid to scare it, she just stood there. "It's not going anywhere," her grandfather told her. Sometimes Jenny thought he knew everything about animals, even what they were thinking.

"How come he's not with the rest of the butterflies in the old maple?" Jenny questioned the old man.

"Not all animals belong together, Jenny," he answered her.

And every day after that the Butterfly came to the windowsill. Sometimes only for a while, but he always came. It puzzled Jenny because he never joined the others.

One morning she asked her grandfather, "Should we take him to the others in the old maple?"

"No," replied the old man. "Just because he doesn't have any butterfly friends doesn't mean he doesn't have friends. The Butterfly has us. Even if we are different from him, we can still be his friends."

Jenny remembered this all her life. Many years after her grandfather died she realized what he was trying to tell her. It doesn't matter if your friends are different from you, they can still be the most important people in your life.

THE DOLL SHOP

by

CARLEE HOBBS

age 12

It was summer again, and my family was moving. I guess I was glad, I didn't really have any friends here in Seattle. We were moving to a small town about an hour north of Seattle called Minnow Creek.

I'm ten, and my name is Mariah Lecksly. I have a mom, a dad, and a little sister named Elizabeth (Beth).

The trip to Minnow Creek had been long and boring. Beth had constantly been yelling in my ear to play dolls with her. So after unpacking, I was happy to go exploring. The girl from next door was knocking at the door.

"Hi! I'm Sarah. I live over there," she pointed to a blue-and-cream house to the right of ours. "I came to see if you wanted to come with me downtown, and I could show you around." Sarah smiled welcomingly.

"Um, sure, let me ask," I answered, a bit awed at her enthusiastic manner.

"Mother?" I asked, approaching her as she finished unpacking the kitchen. "The girl next door wants to know if I can come with her to the downtown area."

"Of course. Get to know the area before school starts, and meet people," she said, not looking at me. I started toward the door. "Oh, and take Beth with you? That would help a lot and get her out of my hair," she added, examining a broken spatula.

"Ugh," I groaned. I always had to bring her along, the little beast. Beth was just reaching the peak of her terrible twos and was very annoying.

"Me go too! Me go too!" Beth yelled excitedly.

I turned to Sarah. "Is it OK if Beth goes?"

"Sure!" she answered, and looking at Beth, "Aren't you cute!"

I sighed disgustedly. Who would think *Beth* was cute? I decided to change the subject. "How old are you?" I asked.

"I'm eleven," she told me. "How old are you?"

"Ten, so that means we'll be in different grades," I said. That disappointed me because so far I liked Sarah. "Let's get going," I said, and after I grabbed Beth's hand, the three of us headed for Main Street.

By the time we reached Main Street, I was huffing. In Seattle, you barely had to walk to get into the business section. You either rode the bus, or the store was just next door. I figured I should question Sarah about this. "Are there any buses in Minnow Creek?" I asked out loud.

"Nope," she answered.

Oh, I thought. I'm going to have to get into shape.

Sarah was talking. "See, over there is the café. And over there is the bookstore, my favorite. To the left is the grocery store, and to the right is the department store. Oh, and way over there on the corner is The Doll Shop."

The Doll Shop! I love dolls. My whole room is filled with dolls of all kinds, even though I am getting somewhat old for dolls, I mean, ten. People would laugh if they knew! I decided to tell Sarah anyway. "Oh, let's go there! I just love dolls!" I practically yelled, trying to contain my excitement.

"Um, uh, let's not and say we did," she stuttered nervously.

"Are you afraid?" I asked, curious and amazed.

"Can you keep a secret?" she questioned. I answered yes. I pride myself in keeping my friends' secrets. "I am kind of scared, but wait! I have a reason!" she added, noticing my disapproving look.

"Everyone, well kids mostly, are afraid of her. See, it's said that she puts spells on kids, turning them into dolls. Plus, it's dark and dreary inside," she paused. "Oh, and the adults say, 'There's nothing to be scared of, the place has character,' but you can see in their eyes that they were just as afraid of her when they were kids," she ended her explanation in a whisper, leaving an eerie silence in the air around us.

Even as she told me this, I became even more anxious to get inside of the little shop. My parents tell me I'm exactly like Curious George.

I thought a moment. It seemed that Sarah wouldn't go in there for the world. I came up with a very weird but creative idea. Beth hadn't been listening to Sarah. She was interested in a big shaggy dog pulling its master toward a yellow tabby cat. I whispered into Beth's ear that Sarah knew where a doll shop was. You see, Beth loves dolls even more than I do. And if Sarah saw that Beth really wanted to go, she'd go to The Doll Shop even if she didn't really want to. I could already tell that little kids were one of Sarah's soft spots.

Just as soon as I finished whispering into Beth's ear, she started jumping up and down yelling, "I want to go to The Doll Shop!" Sarah glared at me. She wasn't stupid, she saw what I had done. I felt a little guilty, but I really wanted to get into The Doll Shop, and I knew Sarah wouldn't say no to Beth.

So I just smiled back.

As Beth pulled on Sarah's hand, Sarah finally started toward the door. Walking in the direction of The Doll Shop I wondered what could be so bad about a doll shop? I mean, dolls are supposed to be pretty and nice. Questions, questions, questions.

It was too soon when we reached The Doll Shop. I was getting nervous. I almost didn't want to go in, but I had started it so I lifted my chin, took a deep breath, and turned the doorknob.

I opened the door slowly and took a step in, looking around. I realized my heart was pounding. Sarah was right. It *was* dark in there. Many beautiful dolls lined the walls. The shop was considerably tiny, and stuffed with dolls. All kinds! Different cultures, sizes, and shapes of dolls. Each one had a lifelike expression captured on its face. It would have been a doll lover's dream come true, but the heavy atmosphere deleted the usual sparkle dolls gave me.

"Hello?" I barely whispered, seeing no one in the shop. Beth was already poking around in the dolls. I repeated my question, and this time I got an answer.

"Come in, come in," a raspy voice croaked, and a moment later a small, bent, wrinkled old woman stepped out from the shadows. She wasn't exactly scary looking. Her face had a bright, cheery glow.

"Two of you! And the little cutie!" she exclaimed, smiling.

I groaned inwardly. I'm going to have to get used to this, being new in town. Beth was sure to attract attention by being cute. Ugh. I can't wait! I thought sarcastically.

"Th-th-this is M-m-mariah," Sarah finally was able to get out, stammering. "She just moved here, and I was just showing her around town." It looked as though Sarah was silently pleading to the woman not to turn her into a doll.

Pathetic, I thought, even though the woman didn't notice.

"Ahh," she replied. Staring at Beth she murmured, "What a doll, what a perfect *doll* she is."

Beth hid behind my leg and grinned toothily up at the old woman. The store was nice, but I wanted to get out. "Well, we'd better get going. Nice store you have," I smiled politely and headed for the door. It had sounded as if the woman had said something. I turned around. "What?"

"Oh, I was just telling you that we *do* take trade-ins," she repeated, looking into Beth's clear green eyes.

I saw that Sarah had paled. I think I did too. Now I really wanted to get out of the store! I bolted from the shop with Sarah right behind me. We ran all the way to our street. We were both huffing, from running and from panic. I was the first to speak.

"Oh my gosh, did she mean Beth? Trade Beth in for a doll? I would never do that..." It was then I realized two things. The first thing was how much I loved Beth no matter how much attention she got, and second, *we had left Beth in the store!!* I screamed this out loud. Loud enough that I'm sure my grandparents in Seattle could hear me.

"We've got to go back. I mean, before she..." Sarah said, unable to finish her horrible conclusion.

"...turns her into a doll!" I finished for her.

We both turned and ran at the same time. Sarah and I were about the same speed, mostly because I'm quite tall for my age and the same height as Sarah. I ran as fast as I could, and if anyone had timed me, I would have broken a record. We were at the store in no time.

I burst into the shop, startling Beth and the old woman. The two of them, after glancing up, turned back to what they were doing, playing with dolls. Beth looked as though she was having a good time. After I had stood in the doorway awhile with Sarah, looking at the scene in astonishment, the old woman twisted her head my way and said, "She can have this one if she likes," pointing to a very cute and cuddly doll. "She likes it so much, I won't even make you trade in another."

"What!?" I cried, confused. "You mean, you trade dolls for dolls?"

"Yes, what in heaven's else would I trade?" she questioned, seeming as confused as I was.

A big, *big* misunderstanding. She never meant for me to trade in Beth. I almost laughed out loud. Instead I took a deep breath, realizing I had barely taken a breath since we ran out of the shop.

Everyone reacted a little different. Sarah and I were both relieved. The old woman's expression plainly showed hurt, and Beth was just happily playing with her new doll. The old woman spoke next.

"Don't tell me you believe those witchcraft tales that I trade kids for dolls?" she asked, obviously hurt.

I told the woman that I was happy that a doll shop was in town, and there was nothing to be afraid of, but she looked a bit sad.

"Why are you sad about that?" I asked, dumbfounded.

"You two are basically the only ones in town that aren't afraid of me," she explained. "And my business is running down with no one buying or trading dolls."

I thought a moment. I do a lot of thinking, I just thought. Ha, ha, get it? Anyway, if Sarah and I could spread the word that this woman only trades dolls, her business would probably pick up. I told her this, and she was very grateful. I'm glad too because now there is a good chance that I'll be able to enjoy the store like I originally thought.

"We'd better get going. It's time for lunch and Beth's N-A-P," I said, spelling the word "nap" because if Beth hears that word she'll never go to bed. I also told the woman that we would be back because Beth and I both love dolls.

As Beth, Sarah, and I walked home, my stomach growled. All that excitement, and all before lunch! It was then I decided I would definitely like living in Minnow Creek, even if I always had Beth tagging along!

DANDELION SEEDS

by

MARA GILBERT

age 13

One hot summer day, late in August, Annie was sitting under a large oak. Amy, her friend, sat next to her in the cool grass. Joan, Annie's baby sister, played among a few fallen leaves, trying to catch a little bug that kept hopping away.

"Please take Joan with you, and be sure not to get dirty!" Annie's mother had told them as they left the house. They groaned but were obliged to take her with them.

"Why don't we go to our secret spot?" suggested Amy as they passed the barn full of sweet-smelling hay. They liked their spot. They shared secrets and played games there, like most best friends.

"All right," agreed Annie. "Let's go by way of the forest path." The path through the woods was their favorite way to get to their "spot." It passed over several large rotting logs and a small trickling stream. The big oaks and pines towered above them as they went along. Dried leaves and needles were strewn about over the path and made crackling noises as they walked. It was very cool and wondrous under there.

As they reached the big oak they noticed a large patch of dandelions under the tree. Sitting down they began to talk over the things they had done together earlier that summer. Amy idly picked a dandelion and blew away some of the fluff. Annie waved one in the air; seeds blew everywhere.

"I bet," said Amy, "that you couldn't blow all the fluff off in one breath!"

"I bet I could, too!" retorted Annie.

"All right then," she answered, "but… if you can't, then you have to go home and help your mother."

"I already am helping my mother, by taking care of Joan!"

"Well, if you can… then there's no need to worry."

"All right then," said Annie, picking a flower, then taking a deep breath, "I bet I can!" She blew long and hard, blowing seeds everywhere. Joan sneezed.

"Seee!" said Annie, showing the bare flower head to her friend. "What did I tell you?"

"You mean what did I tell you! Look," answered Amy, "there's one tuft sticking out that you didn't blow off!"

"Oooops!" giggled Annie. They both laughed.

"Come on, I'll help you with your chores." They raced down the path, swinging Joan between them.

FRIENDS TO THE END

by

HARRY TOPALIAN

age 14

It was a normal day at the Miami Airport.
Crowds of people were moving about in different directions.
A boy of thirteen with dark brown hair feathered back and a
slim body came in with two large suitcases looking nervously
as he walked into the airport. His name was Kenny Peters.
Kenny checked in his luggage and went to gate seventeen for
New York. Sitting down alone he put his elbows on his knees,
chin in hands, and thought back a week to when he had stood
watching his home burn to the ground with his mother, father, and brother inside. The memory was too painful—he
dismissed it.

Today was Wednesday. A week from Monday he would
be starting school in a new town and state. He was always a
loner in his other school. He thought he would be here as well.
I don't care, he thought to himself. He did deep down but
wouldn't admit it. He thought of the Howlands who would
be waiting for him at LaGuardia Airport in New York, and

things didn't seem so bad. He hadn't seen them for a while, but he had nice memories of them.

The plane arrived and everyone boarded. Soon the airplane gave a lurch and taxied down the runway. It took off, wheels going up into their compartments.

The city grew larger as the plane tipped to one side and slid down through the sky. They landed perfectly and the plane pulled up to its gate. Kenny got up and into the line of people departing the plane. He walked past the different terminals and found the gate where the people waited for the passengers of his plane. Faces mixed in the crowd and then he spotted Bob and Thais Howland.

They both were in their early forties, in good physical shape. Bob was tall and dressed sporty, Thais was short with curly hair. After the hugs and hellos, they stood waiting as different bags went around until Kenny spotted his two. The parking lot was full of cars and it took a while to get out.

During the drive, Kenny noticed the amount of trees in Connecticut—there were so many and, of course, different from Florida's.

They finally got off at exit forty-two, Westport/Weston. The sky was a fiery blaze against the top of tall trees, with a glowing yellow-white in the center then to orange, pink, and then a purple with the night beyond waiting to come. "We'll be in Weston in ten minutes," Bob called back to Kenny, who was resting his head against the window, starting to doze. They drove a little farther until they reached Merry Lane. The house was the same as he last saw it three years ago.

Kenny started up the stairs that led to the familiar guest room. Bob called to him, "Get settled, and when you're ready come down to the patio, pool, and food." He rested, put his things away in drawers left empty for them, changed into his bathing suit, and grabbed a towel from the liner closet on the way downstairs. On the patio, Bob was grilling a steak and Thais was on a chaise. The pool felt inviting after the hot day. They ate at the picnic table and afterward went down to the basement to play pool and the video system. Kenny, exhausted from the tiring day, went to sleep early with no trouble.

As his eyes opened the sun was brightly glowing through the room. The small alarm clock on the table in back of him said twelve noon. Looking out the window he could see Bob in the backyard cleaning leaves from the pool. Going downstairs he joined Thais who was in the family room watching a game show. After the "how did you sleep," etc., she fixed him breakfast. She joined him with coffee and conversation.

"When does school start?" Kenny asked.

"A week from Monday—after breakfast why don't we go shopping for school needs."

Inside the mall there were many people. They went from store to store and had quickly bought all the things for school and went to Waldenbooks to get a pocketbook. After Kenny picked it out he went over to the comic book rack which was against a wooden magazine holder. There was a blond boy kneeling at the rack. He looked up as they came over and then back down to the video game magazine he was looking at. The boy was dressed in jeans and a denim jacket. Kenny found some comic books he liked and he lingered, waiting to meet this boy. The boy seemed to be doing the same thing. He, too, looked at the comics. The boy kept moving his small dark yellow bag as people walked by.

"Are you about ready?" Thais asked.

"Just a few more minutes," he said nervously.

The boy walked over to the other side of the rack. Kenny tried turning the rack and it was stuck. The boy helped turn it. Kenny so badly wanted to say something and couldn't. The boy looked at one of the books which Kenny was reading and

Kenny decided that he had to say something—he may never see this boy again. Kenny could feel he liked him—and that the boy would like him in return.

"Do you collect those?" Kenny asked.

He looked up at Kenny. "No, but I buy them sometimes."

There was silence between them.

"I'm Kenny."

"Jeff," said the blond boy who now stood up. They were both about the same height.

"Are you here alone?"

"Yeah, my mom dropped me off."

"Where do you live?" Kenny asked.

"In Weston."

"You're kidding, me too, on Merry Lane."

"I live on Lyons Plains Road."

When Thais wanted to leave, the two boys exchanged phone numbers and said goodbye.

Later in the afternoon, Jeff came over to Kenny's and the Howlands' house. Jeff said he was sorry about Kenny's family and hoped by bringing it up it didn't upset him too much. Kenny told him he was glad he came. He also added that kids our age couldn't care enough to ask about each other's problems. "We're not like most kids, I don't think," said Jeff. Kenny agreed.

The television was on with a news broadcast. "Today, there was an incident of three mutants, technically called homo-superior beings, hunted by a group of vigilantes who have already killed many of these mutants. These three were found bullet-ridden in an alley. The mayor of New York has been in conference as to whether to allow such beings to roam free or to use them for study."

Both boys changed into swimsuits, went downstairs and out to the pool. They sat on the edge of the pool with their feet in the water.

"So what's the school like here?" Kenny asked.

"I don't like it here; the kids aren't really that nice. I just hang around by myself most of the time." Jeff sounded unhappy and that made Kenny feel the same.

"Well, it won't be like that anymore. I was the same way in my old school."

"You had no friends either?" Jeff asked.

"None. They seemed to feel something about me. That's why I'm so glad we're friends already."

"Me too," Jeff said. "Kenny, did you ever hear about mutants?"

"Yeah, why?"

"There was one here on your street and somebody killed her."

"Sounds scary."

"I don't think we've got anything to worry about," Jeff said laughing.

That week they enjoyed each other's company—playing cards, talking, becoming more comfortable with each other as the days passed. Before you knew it Sunday (the last day before school starts) came—the time they both dreaded. Kenny spent the day and night at Jeff's so they could go to school together. That night they each felt the same way—nervous and finding it difficult to get to sleep. The one consolation they each had was they were going to be in a lot of classes with each other.

Morning came, they got up and got ready for school. Neither had breakfast. They left for the bus stop. Three boys on the bus kept harassing them and fear mixed with anger was in them both. When the bus was emptying at Weston Middle School, one of the boys pushed Kenny into Jeff and they both fell to the sidewalk. A strange green van pulled into the schoolyard. Kenny's rage became incredible. He stood up and his body began to shake. "You better leave me and my friend alone or I'll..." His hand, which pointed at the boy, crackled and he looked at it in awe. Energy leaped and danced forth, striking the boy. He fell. Children were running and screaming. Jeff, too, was amazed. The other two went for Kenny when he turned his back to them, and Jeff's mind screamed, I can't let them do it! Instantly, their minds were destroyed. Jeff got up and grabbed Kenny. They both ran in fear of what they had done and what was to happen now. The van followed. They hid in the woods, out of sight.

"What are we?" screamed Kenny.

"I don't know but we can't be human," Jeff answered. "What are we going to do now?"

"I don't know, Jeff, maybe leave Connecticut. We don't fit in here."

"We won't anywhere else either," Jeff said.

They sat on a tree stump pressed tightly together for courage. That was how they were the whole day. At night there were many noises and then one was not just a falling twig. Three people stood before them with loaded guns.

"Well, well, if it isn't two muties," said the woman leading them.

"Please don't hurt us," they said.

"Don't you worry yourselves, we'll kill you quickly. "

No! Jeff screamed in his mind.

She dropped. The other two opened fire. Kenny's attack was too late. Jeff's head fell to his lap.

"Jeff—NO!!!" he sobbed. He looked deeply into his best and only friend's eyes. He had taken three shots. He was drenched in sweat, and tears ran down his face. "Jeff, don't leave me—I need you, you need me, we're best friends—remember!"

"Of course, I do; you're the best, Kenny, I need you, too.

Hold me please." They moved to the ground. Kenny put his arms around Jeff and he put his hand on Kenny's arm.

Kenny put his face in Jeff's hair and cried as Jeff's hand fell to his lap, "FRIENDS—TO THE END!"

There's Nothing Like a Friend

by

Brook Bassett

age 13

Chelsea Taylor sat on the front porch of her house at 203 South Maple. She was wondering what she was going to do all summer. She knew she wouldn't have had any trouble thinking of things to do if she were back in Wisconsin with all her best friends.

Chelsea had just moved from Huntington, Wisconsin, to, in her opinion, ugly Hume City, New York. Her father had been transferred there by the company he worked for. Chelsea hated having to move, but most of all she hated to leave her best friends behind. She especially hated leaving Angie. She had spent many long summer days with Angie for as far back as she could remember.

Chelsea glanced around her new neighborhood and thought to herself. Why did we have to move this year, out of all the years we could have moved? Why did it have to be this year, my first year of junior high? All the kids here will have friends that they grew up with and I'll be on my own. It's so hard making new friends. She slumped against the porch railing. Just the thought of all her friends in Wisconsin brought tears to her eyes. She tried hard to keep from crying, but it was impossible the way it hurt so badly.

She angrily brushed the tears from her eyes as she heard her mother calling.

"Chelsea, would you like some lemonade? It's awfully hot out there."

Chelsea shrugged and abruptly stood up. She walked into the kitchen to find her mom had already poured the glass of lemonade for her. "I'm so bored," she complained to her mother.

"Why don't you go exploring?" her mother suggested. "We've only been here for a week. There has to be a lot you haven't seen yet."

Chelsea sighed. "I did that yesterday and what kind of exploring can you do around here anyway? There are only houses as far as you can see."

"Why don't you go across the street and get acquainted with the girl I saw there earlier? She looks about your age and she might be just as lonely as you," her mother tried to humor her.

"She probably already has a bunch of friends."

"Oh nonsense," replied Mrs. Taylor. "Everyone can use another friend."

Chelsea was not in the mood for all her mother's suggestions. She got up from her chair, took her lemonade, and walked out the door and sat on the porch again. It seemed to her she was spending an awful lot of time on that porch. She glanced across the street to find the neighbor girl was also sitting outside. The girl glanced up at that moment and smiled. Chelsea smiled back and hung her head and sat down. Chelsea was not what you would call outgoing about meeting people. The next ten minutes were spent watching the ants climb the edge of the house.

"Well, this is just a waste of my time," Chelsea muttered to herself as she jumped up. She thought, If that girl isn't going to come over here and I'm too scared to go over there, I'll just have to go in the house. I have a book I could finish anyway. She glanced across the street as she opened the door. The girl was sitting, with her head down, playing with something on the ground.

Chelsea went in the door and went through the kitchen. She climbed the stairs to her room and slowly entered. She went to the bookshelf and took out her book. She sat back in her desk chair with her feet propped up on the bed and opened the book to start reading. It just seemed like words on a page that made no sense at all. After several minutes, she gave up trying to read and went downstairs to see what her mom was doing. Her mother was busy filling a bookshelf with some books that hadn't been unpacked yet. She told Chelsea to grab another box and help out. Oh well, Chelsea thought, it was better than doing nothing.

At 204 South Maple, Sara Casteel watched as Chelsea went into the house. She was hoping the girl across the street would be someone she could be friends with.

Sara got up from the porch where she was sitting and went into the house. She went over to the television and flipped it on. She threw herself down on the couch and flung her legs up on the coffee table. She flipped through the channels until she came to a sitcom with teenage girls. Her mind started to wander. She was thinking of her friends in Ely, Nevada. It seemed she didn't have a friend in the world without Courtney. She watched longingly as the girls on the sitcom laughed and talked with each other. It only made Sara feel worse knowing she had no one to talk and laugh with. She wished she was still in

Nevada with her friends.

Sara just moved to Hume City a few days earlier. Sara's mom was a nurse who specialized in prenatal care and had transferred to a New York hospital where she could get special training they didn't offer where she was before.

Sara's mom walked through the living room and commented, "Sara, go clean your room and stop moping around."

"I'm not moping," Sara said protectively, "I'm just lonely and bored."

"Well, you won't be bored anymore. Go clean your room like I told you," her mother said with a smug smile on her face. "And if you are so darn lonely, just go across the street and meet the girl over there."

Sara, hot-faced and mad, stomped into her bedroom to clean it. The minute she stepped into her room she wished she could back right out again. Her room looked as if a tornado had hit it. Sara wasn't exactly the organized type and oh, how she wished she could be. She did have a bit of an excuse now though because she wasn't exactly completely unpacked yet. Her mother thought the most important part of being healthy was cleanliness, which included her room too.

Sara sat down on the part of the bed she could see and started thinking about the girl across the street. Oh, how she wished she could have just walked across the street when she was out there and walked right up to her and just said, "Hi." Maybe she would have had the beginning of a friendship. Sara never made friends easily. How would she ever make any friends in junior high? This was going to be the longest summer in her life. She picked up a doll that was beside the bed and sat it in front of her pillow. "Well, Trudy, I guess it's just you and me all summer long."

Tuesday morning Chelsea awoke to the warm sun shining across her bed. She moaned and rolled over to look at the clock. "Seven o'clock!" she muttered. "Someone remind me to put some curtains on those dumb windows." She turned over and tried to go back to sleep, but once she was awake, she was awake for good.

As Chelsea got up to get dressed, she could hear the murmur of her parents talking downstairs. As she walked over to her dresser, she could hear what they were saying.

"I really think Chelsea should get out to meet some kids in the neighborhood. She is always moping around these days," she heard her mother say.

Alex Taylor, her father, answered with, "Oh, I think she just needs time to adjust to the change a little more."

Well, at least Dad understands, Chelsea thought to herself. She grabbed some clothes from her dresser and slammed the drawer shut. It had been a week since she had seen the girl across the street. She had been thinking about it for a while now and had decided she needed to work up the courage to cross the street, knock on the door, and introduce herself. After all, she couldn't spend the whole summer in the house.

Chelsea went downstairs for a breakfast of sausage and eggs. When she was finished, she went out to the garage to decide how she was going to attempt the introduction. She thought she could ride her bike up and down the street and then just casually ride up to the girl's house.

Chelsea was really nervous, so nervous she started cleaning her garage. This was getting her nowhere. She jumped up and sat on her father's workbench to think. She started to go over her "maybe list," as she always did when she was going to meet someone new. Maybe the girl wouldn't like her (a very popular one on Chelsea's list). Maybe she wouldn't like the girl. Maybe the girl would ignore her when she rode up. That would be very embarrassing. Maybe the girl wasn't home. Maybe she was too young or too old for her. Oh, so many things could go wrong and it was hard to think of them all. She looked across the workbench and saw a book she had left there. Sometimes reading helped calm her nerves...

Across the street Sara was eating her breakfast of pancakes and juice. Her mother was standing by the stove pouring the last of the batter into the pan. "You know the girl across the street, Mom?" Sara asked.

"Yes, I've seen her around. She looks about your age," Mrs. Casteel replied.

"I've decided to go over and meet her today. I'm so tired of being in the house and if I don't make the first move I might never have a friend before summer ends."

Mrs. Casteel was happy to hear this. She was tired of seeing Sara mope around the house. It was a waste of energy feeling sorry for yourself, she had wisely told Sara the day before. Sara didn't have a father at home to tell her she only needed to get used to the adjustment. Her father had died when she was eight, which left Sara more shy than usual.

Sara had chores to do before she could leave the house. She cleared the table of the dishes and rinsed them and put them in the dishwasher. Then, she went back to her room to make her bed and pick up the clothes she had worn the day before off the floor. All the time she was mechanically doing this, she was thinking of the trip across the street. She decided she would ride her bike over there and then maybe they could go for a bike ride to warm up to each other. That might take the pressure off them both.

Sara went out to the garage to work up her courage. She paced back and forth, wringing her hands and thinking. After several minutes of pacing, she finally sat down on a box that hadn't been unpacked yet. She noticed it was marked "Sara."

She supposed she could unpack it. As she ripped open the box, she thought of all the things that could go wrong meeting the girl across the street. Maybe Sara wouldn't like her or worse yet, maybe the girl wouldn't like Sara. Maybe the girl was stuck up or had too many friends already. Maybe she just plain wouldn't want to be her friend or maybe...

After an agonizing hour at both houses, Chelsea and Sara both had had enough. They each jumped on their bicycles at the same time and started pedaling from their garages. Both houses sat on a hill and both driveways led to the street. Both girls sped down the driveways without another thought, so they wouldn't be able to change their minds. Cruising pretty fast, they both glanced up at the same time halfway down.

"Oh, no!" cried Chelsea.

"Watch out!" screamed Sara.

Unable to stop, both faces expressed their terror. But it was too late. Both girls put on their brakes to try and stop, but not in time. They ran smack into each other, falling to the ground like bundles of laundry, heavy laundry. Both girls burst out laughing.

"Are you all right?" Chelsea asked between giggles.

"Yeah, how about you?" Sara managed to get out.

"I'm OK."

Both girls started to talk excitedly at once.

"That was fun. Want to do it again?"

"Not right away, I don't think. Maybe later."

Giggling, they both said together, "Not!"

Looks like it's going to be a great summer after all, both girls thought to themselves.

FANTASIZING EMMA

by

SARA HAHN

age 13

I hate my name. Emma. How many people are there in the world named Emma? Too many. Obviously no one gets credit for naming their poor me something original—something that not everyone has. Something like Meredith, or Lara, or Aisling. But not Emma. I've always been a little proud of myself for having some qualities that make me a well-rounded person—my good grades, athletic abilities, and having some great friends. Those great friends happen to be very close school companions—Christie, Eileen, and Allison. I'm always grateful for them and many other characteristics of myself, and I'm proud. But I can't be proud of my name. I've always wanted to change it but never was given the opportunity. Not until Tuesday.

It was late spring. Temperate weather had made its brief interlude for the first time in months; the sun was warming our shoulders, invigorating us after the long and gray winter.

It was a Tuesday afternoon at school. Christie, Eileen, Allison, and I were sitting together under a tree, watching our fellow sixth-graders as they engaged in the procedure of a typical school day: food throwing, arguing, and disobeying the teachers. Allison had smuggled her Walkman onto the campus and now she and Eileen were debating over which CD to play. Christie and I had been appointed Lookout People, so whenever a teacher headed in our direction, we could warn Allison to hide the Walkman. I was tired and just watching the lazy clouds as they moved at a sluggish pace across the azure sky.

"Oh man, Allison, a teacher's coming!" I heard Eileen exclaim. I brought myself to a more appropriate sitting position to see Allison shoving her slew of CDs and the Walkman under Christie's backpack.

"Weren't you guys on the lookout?!" she hissed as the teacher approached us.

It was Miss Humbert, whose stern and easily annoyed personality made her regarded by the students as, well, bad. She worked yard duty and was never familiar with any of the students—actually, she didn't even know our names. Her dark hair hung in a limp wave that fell a little above her jaw, a jaw set rigid and narrow. She scowled at us with dull, brown eyes.

"OK," Miss Humbert said to us in her low, gruff voice, "hand over your little... recorder."

"It isn't a... recorder," Allison muttered as she thrust the Walkman at the teacher. Allison had a naturally aggressive temper and I could tell it was about to blow, like a volcano under pressure.

Christie, Eileen, and I remained quiet, while a red-faced Allison glowered at Miss Humbert, who was lecturing, "You know the rules. You, Miss..." she glared at Allison "...have disobeyed our school's rules." At that, I began to feel a little awkward. It was true, we had disobeyed.

"All of you girls don't know how dangerous this equipment can be."

Despite my mild guilt, I had to try not to laugh with the other girls—the thought of a Walkman being dangerous!—and then Allison said through clenched teeth, "Oh yeah, sure, especially now that the yard duty teacher has contaminated it."

That did it. All four of us burst out laughing. With a steaming red face and flaring eyes, Miss Humbert said, "Fine, ladies, if this is how you wish to behave, I'm going to write you up for an after-school detention with the principal. You may all stay for an extra hour and a half starting at three o'clock this Friday."

We became deathly silent. I heard Allison groan. Serve *detention?* I couldn't do that! I was an overall good student; I usually obeyed the teachers. But now my reputation would be completely ruined! I sunk low to the ground, wishing it would suck me up.

Miss Humbert drew a pen from her pocket and poised it above her clipboard. Allison looked ready to protest, but Miss Humbert inquired hastily, "Now, tell me your names."

It was then that something clicked inside of Allison. I, along with Christie and Eileen, could practically see her mind developing a devilish little plan, and everyone under that tree was getting prepared for it.

Everyone but Miss Humbert, so that when Allison chirped politely, "My name is Melissa Corgan," the teacher said, "Thank you, Melissa."

I stifled my gasp. Miss Humbert didn't know our names! If she reported the fake one Allison had just made up, well then, we would be off the hook, just like that!

"My name is Amber... Anderson," Eileen told Miss Humbert.

I thought of a name quickly: Allegra Mercedes. When

Miss Humbert asked my name, I would say... Allegra Mercedes. It would be OK, right? I was sensing a fear inside of me. It wasn't wrong to be lying about our names, right?

A cascade of thoughts showered upon me. Here was my chance to have a different name, a name I had always been wanting. Now I could have any name I liked, as creative and as unusual as I wanted. I wouldn't have to be boring Emma Robinson anymore. I could be any person I wanted! But was it wrong to do so?

It will be OK, I assured myself. Don't worry about lying, and anyway, you're going to get out of an after-school detention.

"I'm Kristen Banderas," Christie swallowed abruptly.

Allison looked ready to burst out laughing, but I couldn't help the guilt that was now building inside of me. Here I was, Emma Robinson, about to become another person. I had fantasized about having another name, but not because I had committed a serious school offense.

Why had I done it? Why hadn't I just told Allison to put the Walkman away so we wouldn't all be in such trouble? If anyone found out that my friends and I were lying about our names, we would be in worse trouble than what we started off with.

Miss Humbert was scrawling in her notebook. Just hearing the pen against paper made me feel uneasy. "And your name?" she asked me gruffly.

It was now or never. Should I choose a name I had always wanted? Who was I?

"My name is Em... Emily," I said feeling my tense heart throb. I had almost said that my name was Emma! "Emily... Smith."

The teacher nodded at us. "Very well, all of you—um—" she looked at her clipboard in reference—"Melissa, Amber,

Kristen, Emily—come to the principal's office after school on Friday. You'll stay there for an hour and a half. Show these slips to your parents; I want them returned to the principal tomorrow. I'll return the Walkman at the end of the school year, and don't argue about it." She tore off four slips of paper from her clipboard and handed them to each of us, then left.

I scrutinized the paper in apprehension; I had never received a detention slip before. It was teeming with fine print, and at the bottom was written, "Parent or guardian's signature is requested here. I agree that my son/daughter, Emily Smith, will serve one and a half hours of detention this Friday, April 14."

"Allison," I groaned, "Allison, we're busted! Our parents have to sign these, and if my mom and dad find out what we just did, they'll be kind of upset..."

"Relax, Emily," Allison said, smiling fiendishly, "our parents aren't even going to find out about this. Remember, these detention slips give names that don't exist—well, not at this school. We won't even have to show them to our parents. And since the principal won't know who these detentions are really for, we won't have to show, and we'll be just fine!"

I laughed nervously, trying to release my uneasiness. It would have been the perfect plan; but I knew what we had done was wrong.

And after school, when I went home, I still felt aching remorse. I hid in my bedroom upstairs as if it were the sanctuary and I the refugee. I really shouldn't have been so inconsiderate to Miss Humbert, I thought. But—if I were to serve detention, Mom and Dad would be upset, and I would be letting Allison down, I countered. And I might lose some of my reputation, and I would be embarrassed.

But what if I didn't serve detention? I reasoned. Well, I would be guilt-ridden for a long time. I wouldn't be letting Allison or my friends down, but I would be letting myself down. If I did, I could discharge my awful feelings of guilt and live up to what I had done. If I didn't, I would… now I couldn't think of any more reasons.

I really was Emma Robinson, and even my fake name didn't disguise what I had done. I had always fantasized about having another name, but being Emily Smith didn't make me proud.

I knew what to do. I grabbed a pen from my desk and scratched out where Miss Humbert had written Emily Smith on the detention slip. Before I went downstairs to talk to my parents, I wrote clearly and carefully, Emma Robinson.

A TRUE
FRIEND

by

JENNIFER L. CASWELL

age 10

"And guess what she said," Jessi snickered. Everyone but me gazed eagerly at her. I squeezed my eyes shut. I had joined the "popular" group about a month ago and still hadn't gotten used to it. They had accepted me, although I would never know why.

My friends and I were at what was supposed to be the best sleepover Jessi had ever had. We were scattered around the tile floor of her basement in our sleeping bags, listening to one of her stories about Jasmine. In the short time I'd been friends with Jessi I'd grown used to these stories. I knew every lie that had ever fallen from Jasmine's lips.

"She says, 'Jess, I am so good at ice skating, I can do a triple axel,'" Jessi finished. The people around me broke into peals of laughter. I forced a grin onto my embarrassed face. It just didn't seem fair to talk about people that way behind their backs. Besides, I was exhausted and wanted to plop down on my pillows and collapse.

"Tell us more, tell us more," the other girls squealed. I covered my head with my hands and wished they would vanish into thin air.

"Lori hasn't said anything. You should make her tell you a story," Jessi said smugly. I gasped. Was this Jessi's way of testing me to see if I was ready to be "popular"?

"Yeah, Lori, Lori, Lori," the crowd around me started to chant. I searched my mind frantically. I couldn't make fun of anyone. And anyway, I didn't know anything about Jasmine to tell!

"Nah," I mumbled. "Make Sally tell a story. I like listening more." I was sure they would persist, but they didn't. Sally took advantage of her moment in the spotlight to begin a story. I silently thanked her.

My father and I set out the next morning for grocery shopping. "Milk," he told me. I knew my whole job for that morning was to load myself with milk, bring it back to the cart, load myself with milk again, and bring it back to the cart again, etc. Dad pushed the cart over to the yogurt section.

My parents are obsessed with calcium.

On one of my many trips between cart and milk, I saw Jasmine and her mother. I paused, almost dropping my three milk cartons. (One in each of my hands and one on my head. I *did* drop the one on my head.) I put all of them down, except the one I dropped, and that I placed upright and crept closer. This, I told myself, could be my chance to get a story to tell Jessi and prove myself worthy of the popular crowd.

But the story I heard was not one I would ever repeat. It struck me ice cold in the heart. Jasmine and her mother were leaning over the candy bin.

"Lemon drops falling from the sky. Gumdrops coming too," sang Jasmine in a perfect voice.

"Shut up, child!" her mother whispered angrily. "Someone might hear your awful voice. Now Jason, would you like another chess set?" She smiled at Jasmine's brother. I suddenly remembered that Jason was a chess prodigy. My heart was suddenly filled with pity for Jasmine. For a split second I hated Jessi and the crowd. For a split second.

The next school day my group and I walked to school together. We laughed about Jasmine and a few other "nerds," as we popular kids called them. With my friends I seemed to be able to joke about people without feeling embarrassed. When Jasmine skipped by, we all stifled our giggles and acted calm. Except me. Upon seeing her, I suddenly remembered what I had seen at the grocery store the day before.

"I'm sorry Jasmine," I muttered and ran away before anyone could see my tears.

As I fled away I realized what a fool I had made of myself. What was wrong with me? The first good friends I got and I totally embarrassed myself in front of them. "Oh come on Lori, don't be dumb! Jasmine will never know if you tease her behind her back. Oh please, just try to be like them." I needed friends more than anything else. Well, if my friends liked making fun of Jasmine, making fun of Jasmine it would be!

It was a beautiful spring morning. The birds were chirping in the trees, the sun was shining down on the tulips, and the world was glistening with dew. Our whole bunch was down by the creek, watching the tadpoles dart around. Jessi was complaining that it was boring, and everyone else was agreeing. Except for me, of course, who would rather stay on the riverbank forever than go throw some dumb ball. But I wasn't about to disagree, so I followed them up the steps and over to the blacktop.

"All right," Sally began. "Who's on whose team?"

Slowly, we divided into teams for basketball. It was four against five. My team was short by one person, and I was a hindrance to them. When they passed to me (if I caught it), I would shoot at the wrong basket. If I caught a pass and didn't go to the basket we were defending, I would usually give the ball to the other team. No, we couldn't go on like this. We needed one more girl, and she had to be *good*.

Jasmine came over from the hopscotch. "I see you need one more person. And I'm mighty good," she said proudly.

I wasn't sure what to say. After all, if what Jessi said was true, Jasmine was lying. Nonetheless, we needed someone else, and Jasmine did say she was good...

I soon found out I didn't have a say in the matter. My teammates were already murmuring among themselves.

"We can't let her play, she sucks," Jessi whispered.

"As if Lori doesn't," another kid hissed. I decided to pretend I hadn't heard.

"Hey," I said. "If she's bad, and I'm bad, why not have her on one team and me on the other? We'll cancel each other out."

The kid who had said I couldn't play blushed but nodded her agreement. "All right," Jessi decided. "Jasmine, you are on their team. Casey," she said, pointing to a short, brown-haired girl on the other team, "you're on ours."

Our opponents groaned. They didn't want any more than Jessi had to have Jasmine on their team.

The game flew by. I, as always, scored the other team two points and gave them a couple of foul shots. Although Jasmine didn't do anything despicable, like me, she didn't help her team much. It was almost as if she wasn't there. Nevertheless, they won, 22 to 12. It seemed that whatever team I was on, lost. That made sense.

What didn't make sense, though, was that Jasmine lied. Maybe all of Jessi's stories were true. I felt anger steaming up inside me. I hated liars.

Soon after our basketball game, the bell pierced the air. We all scrambled inside, hoping our music teacher had suddenly died of pneumonia. Nope. Mrs. Smith was there, half smiling, half sneering at us when we got in the room. I wanted to run out of the room when I saw her face with the ice-cold marbles staring at me. I always do. It suddenly struck me. If I was frightened, what was Jasmine? She had always seemed like a scared person.

I sang first. Our song was one that went terribly high so that my voice creaked, squeaked, and then collapsed at the end.

Jessi rolled her eyes when it was her turn. The teacher didn't seem to notice. Sometimes I wish I was brave like Jessi. I want to be able to laugh in the face of danger, the way she does.

Then it was Jasmine's turn. The teacher nodded at her, the cue to begin. She didn't start. Jasmine froze right in her position. Her mouth seemed to open and close. Every time it was like she hoped for something to come out, but nothing ever did. Everyone turned and gaped at her. No one, no one ever stopped singing in front of Mrs. Smith. She was quite strict when it came to that, and one of her rules was, "Always participate in musical activities." Jasmine, everyone knew, was in for it.

Mrs. Smith stood up to her full, imposing height. "I want to hear you sing," she bellowed. Jasmine opened her mouth, but not a word came out.

"Are you deaf? Mute? Sing child!" As Mrs. Smith said this, Jasmine's face turned beet red.

"I, I, I w-w-want t-to," Jasmine stammered. I could tell she was going to cry, but I yearned for her not to. I sat in my hard, yellow chair and tried to send telepathic rays of courage to her.

"Then do," Mrs. Smith said harshly.

Jasmine croaked the song out, but she sounded dreadful. Worse than I had, and that was hard.

"Good, I'm glad I don't have to report you to the principal," Mrs. Smith said. I don't really think she would have reported Jasmine to the principal. Mrs. Smith is known for trying to scare people.

I couldn't wait until recess. Social studies went by in a flash, although that might have been because I wasn't paying any attention. I was imagining how lucky I was to have such perfect friends who would play with me at recess.

When lunch break came, I gobbled up my food. Recess came quickly and everyone poured outside, my friends and I discussing whose ball we were going to use for some game that I had never played before. Apparently, Jessi's ball was the smoothest, but Casey's was bluest.

After a while of playing with Jessi's ball, I excused myself. "I gotta go," I announced. Everyone laughed as if I had just made a hilarious joke. I went inside feeling like a hero.

As I entered the bathroom I heard the most sweet singing. It was "Simple Gifts." I tiptoed over to where I thought it was coming from, making sure I wasn't making any noise. I knocked gently on the door. Jasmine came hastily out.

"Oh no, you're one of those girls, aren't you?" she said saucily. Although she acted as if she were angry, she looked more like a frightened rabbit. I felt like she would dart away from me any minute. I wanted to say that I wouldn't hurt her, but that sounded too childish.

"Well, yes, I guess so..." I trailed off.

"And you've come on a bet, right, to see if you could scare me, right?" Now I could tell by her eyes that she was terrified. I could see her tension. It probably had happened before. My friends would do that sort of thing. Suddenly I realized what my friends were. I shuddered at the thought. At least I wasn't doing anything as cruel as that.

"Oh no, I hadn't the faintest idea you were here." I smiled weakly.

"Good, I guess..." she muttered in a way that told me she didn't trust me.

"Well, um," I stuttered, trying to think of something to say. "You sing very well." I had a feeling I wasn't going to get anywhere.

She shook her head. "No I don't."

"But you do!" I said, meaning it.

"No I don't," she repeated.

"You sing beautifully, you can't deny it."

"My mother doesn't think so."

Your mother is a stupid, rotten person, I wanted to say. But I didn't. "I know," was all I managed.

"You know, I hate my mother."

"I can see why," I said under my breath. She apparently heard me.

"And I hate you! I hate you all! Your whole point in life is making mine harder for me. Don't you know what I go through? Don't you care? I hate you. I hate me for hating you. I hate me for hating my mother. I hate *you* for hating my mother. I hate this whole world! I especially hate myself!"

Suddenly I had an urge to hug her. And unlike everything else I had thought to say or do, I decided to. I threw my arms around her and squeezed.

Jasmine sniffled a little, and then she was calm. "I'm sorry," she muttered.

"It's OK." I felt as if a huge weight had been lifted off my back. I understood Jasmine, but more importantly, I understood myself. I realized why I'd wanted to be with Jessi and the crowd. It was because I had no one else. But now I did. I had Jasmine. As I looked at her I realized that she understood. She understood everything.

You can never choose a best friend, they kind of just come to you, and you come to them. I had come to Jasmine that one time in the bathroom, but really, she had come to me.

A Christmas Secret

by

Laura Chaddock

age 11

"Let's do it again," Drew pleaded. "I've never had so much fun in my life."

"This time you push me down," Steve remarked, his blue eyes wide with excitement, while rubbing his hands together to fight off the bitter cold.

"I wish my mom would get me an orange sled, too," Drew frowned and carefully picked up a handful of snow, sticking it into his open mouth, "and a Power Ranger, Nintendo, and a bike..." Drew had never had a warm, happy family. The eight-year-old used to wish a lot; he believed that if you wished enough, the wishes would come true. Every year, he asked Santa Claus, the Easter Bunny, even the Tooth Fairy, to bring his parents back together, but it never happened. Last year, he stopped believing in them. Then, he started to think that everyone would let him down. Every night, Drew would sit in his dark, small house waiting to hear his mother, a waitress, unlock the front door. He would run to give her a hug, but she just pushed him aside, whisking back her long, black hair and asking if her coffee were ready yet. Drew wished that she would ask him if her bear hugs from him were ready yet. Drew needed a lot of love to fill up his empty heart.

Steve smiled. "Come on. Soon my mom will have the hot chocolate ready. You can even go down the hill next," he remarked and rubbed his woolen gloves together. For a second his blue eyes looked a little guilty.

Happily, Drew jumped onto the sled and with a big push was soon at the other end of Steve's yard. When Drew started hauling the sled back up the hill, Steve's face turned red and motioned for Drew to stop. He was pointing at something under his holly bush. He had put on his coonskin cap and was staring at a small, curly haired object, with stout legs and a big, wet nose. Drew ran up the hill and froze next to him.

"It's a dog," he whispered.

"Wow," Drew mumbled. He looked at Steve and smiled. The dog was shaking as it played with a berry it had found on the ground.

"I wonder if it's lost," Steve murmured.

"It isn't wearing a collar," Drew pointed out.

Steve whistled. Drew patted his leg and whispered, "Here boy!" The dog's head jerked toward them, and a second later all that was left of him were four foggy footprints, as he dashed down the street.

Steve shrugged. "Dogs never liked me anyway. Oh well —this time you push me."

Drew nodded, looked at the dog's footprints one last time, and gave Steve a small push, getting him just past the first oak tree.

Smiling, Steve ran back and placed his coonskin cap on Drew. "Now Drew, you're Davy Crockett!" the nine-year-old giggled and gave Drew a big push.

Trees flashed by Drew as the wind took the coonskin cap from his head. A blurry figure ran beside the orange sled. Drew turned around and smiled. Wagging his tail, the dog had the cap gripped between his teeth.

Steve liked to see Drew smile. "Hey!" he exclaimed, running down the hill. "That's mine!" Laughing, he started to run after the stray dog, screaming, "Come on, Drew! You can get him!"

Finally, the dog plopped down in the wet snow and started wagging his tail. Steve grabbed the cap and stuck it back on his head. "Now I'll have doggie slobber all over my hair!" he stiffly remarked, but he was smiling.

Drew reached out to touch the dog's head and he licked his hand. Drew smiled again and whispered, "You're a good boy."

"Drew! Steve! Hot chocolate! Come on, the marshmallows are already in it!" Mrs. LaMont yelled from Steve's front door. "Hurry, it's getting cold!"

"Stay here," Steve and Drew warned the dog. "We'll be right back." The dog whimpered as they ran up the steps.

Their new best friend, the white dog, appeared every day that snowy week, sometimes even bringing them surprises that he had found. Steve noticed a lot of smiles on Drew's freckled face that week.

"What should we name the little fellow? We've just called him doggie for the last seven days. He deserves a real name." Steve sighed. The boys were outside while snow flurries were falling. The small dog was hopping around in the snow with Steve's cap in his mouth. Drew was holding the orange sled, catching the snow in his mouth, watching Steve chase the dog around, screaming, laughing, having fun. "Tomorrow is Christmas Eve, too," Steve added. "The cute little guy doesn't have a name yet," he paused, "or a home." He gave the shivering dog a loving look.

Drew pulled his hat down over his ears as he suggested, "We'll name him Curly. Curly," Drew said again, satisfied. "My dad always told me to name something after their looks."

"Curly?" Steve mimicked, scratching the dog's belly. "I was thinking of something more like Misty, since he's as white as mist."

Drew wrinkled his nose to show his disapproval.

Steve's blue eyes looked like he was disappointed that Drew didn't like his name. Then he slowly asked, "But Drew, our..." he searched for the word, "our moms still don't know about Misty. I always tell my mom and dad everything."

"They'll make us give Curly away," Drew sighed.

"Then Misty will be all alone!" Steve shrugged as he watched the dog roll in the wet snow. A smile appeared on his face. "Maybe I can take him home if I can convince my parents."

"But I want him, too!" Drew shot back. "Your family gets to put up a big, pretty Christmas tree, and your grandparents come for a long visit. I only get a few presents, a candy cane, and a pat on the back from my mom! It's not fair!" Drew bit his lip. Silence fell around them as Steve's eyes turned guilty. Drew looked down at his feet and ran inside.

It was Christmas morning. There was blueberry jam still on the corners of Drew's mouth from his breakfast as he skipped down his front steps.

"Merry Christmas, Drew!" Steve smiled and held out a card. "I made it on the computer just for you," he remarked.

From behind Drew's back came a little box. "I made this all by myself," he said proudly. Tearing off the wrapping paper, Steve found a white dog made out of clay. On his red collar it said, "Steve's Misty." He stared at it, his face red. "You can have him," Drew whispered. Then, opening the card from Steve, he read out loud, "To my best eight-year-old friend. To make your holiday happy, take Curly, our best friend, and give him a happy life. From, Steve."

They both looked up and smiled at each other.

SUNSHINE

by

SARA WON

age 12

The moonlight stared down onto the shimmering water and the gentle breeze started to whisper again. The evening was calm, balmy, and had the fragrance of dry grass. Fall was approaching, having left the warm nights of the summer behind. Almost a year now, the streets had become my closest friends. Scrounging for food had taken my spare time and now a dollar was a treasure. Rarely came a full stomach and a warm bed, often an empty stomach and an icy sidewalk were my comfort.

Tonight, however, I was in luck to find a sheltered place to rest. As I gazed up into the sparkling sky, the stars glimmered down on my eyes, winking their light through the shadows. I began to drift off to sleep with the soft hum of crickets in the background.

I awoke to the startling blare of a car horn. The city was again buzzing with people on their way to work. The sun was peeking over the rolling hilltops and casting dim sketches of objects on the horizon. The morning was still early, but I had to get moving before the guards came around. Clouds skimmed the sky, floating lazily along.

When I peered over to the nearest clock, the time read six twenty-seven AM. None of the local mom-and-pop shops would be open yet, and not many people would be wandering the streets. Going to the back of a small restaurant, I quietly used the hose to wash my face and hands. My hair really smelled horrible and I was in need of a shower. While planning out my schedule for the day, I strolled down a back alley and onto a residential street. The trees were neatly trimmed, houses were clean and tidy, and a dim glow of light came from one window in every house. The avenue was picturesque, peaceful. It seemed as if out of a storybook.

I decided to sit and enjoy the fresh, crisp morning air before anyone began to move about. Silence filled my ears, and life at that moment seemed too good to be true. But the perfect life wasn't for me. A door slammed and abruptly broke my wishful trance.

Before the morning became too late, I was in need of breakfast. Slowly rising, I stood from the curb and began a leisurely stroll to an early morning diner. The breeze pushed against my nose and made the tips of my fingers turn a chilling numbness. I sped briskly down the sidewalk as cars whizzed by my ears. Leaves glided through the air as they fell from the bare trees and covered the streets in a sunset. Coming to a stoplight I watched the hurried business people scurrying to their jobs, but there I was, someone with no particular destination, besides breakfast, and calm and relaxed. The light turned green and I crossed to the corner diner.

When I shoved the door open a rush of warmth enveloped me and the sizzling smells of grease filled the room. Clattering was heard in the back and shouts of orders were yelled out. Customers waited anxiously for their food, and chatter hummed from wall to wall. Wonderfully strong smells rose up into the air and tumbled down into the front of the diner, catching me by the nose, then dragging my hunger further. The crinkle of newspapers was heard as relaxed customers sipped coffee and took their time.

A waitress found a spare moment to offer me a seat, but I politely asked if any help was needed in the kitchen. I told her that I would gladly work for a meal. She seemed hesitant, as if I was going to cause trouble. Kindly, she apologized that no help was needed, but breakfast was on the house, just for me. I graciously thanked her and took a seat in the corner. My stomach grumbled as I scanned the menu. Once the waitress came back I was ready to order.

"One stack of pancakes, a side order of bacon, toast, fresh fruit, and one hot chocolate," I muttered, thinking twice about how much I had ordered. The waitress left with a perky smile and rosy cheeks aglow with friendship.

Peering out of the window I saw a faint drizzle begin to shimmer. People scrambled for cover under awnings or suddenly decided to dash for the subway, instead of a leisurely stroll to work. Before long, the drops came down crashing like marbles, pounding against the glass. Puddles formed in the street as cars splashed through them, spraying a fine mist.

My attention was turned to the waitress. She had brought my breakfast, along with a scarf. I turned to thank her, but as if embarrassed, she skipped off to another customer.

I shyly stood and walked out, again bursting into the sharp bite of the chilled air. The city was alive once more with the noise and confusion. The soft drizzle had stopped but the sky loomed with darkness, almost forbidding. In the corner of my eye flashed a patch of sunlight, peeking through the darkness with a strong hope to let its own light shine through all that surrounded it. Just then, my steps quickened, my head lifted, and my eyes showed a glimmer of faith.

CPSIA information can be obtained at www.ICGtesting.com
Printed in the USA
BVOW020617240513

321535BV00007B/136/P

9 780894 090127